DEAR SISTERS,

TWELVE WAYS TO GROW AUTHENTIC COMMUNITY WITH YOUR SISTERS IN CHRIST

Kaye Mayes

Renewed Christian Living

Kaye Mayes/Renewed Christian Living
www.renewedchristianpublishing.com

Publisher's Note:
Unless otherwise indicated, all Scripture quotations are from THE HOLY BIBLE, NEW INTERNATIONAL VERSION®, NIV® Copyright © 1973, 1978, 1984, 2011 by Biblica, Inc.® Used by permission. All rights reserved worldwide. Scripture quotations marked MSG are taken from *The Message*. Copyright © 1993, 1994, 1995, 1996, 2000, 2001, 2002. Used by permission of NavPress Publishing Group. All Scripture quotations marked as ERV are taken from the *Easy to Read Version*. Copyright © 2006 by Bible League international.

Book Layout ©2017 BookDesignTemplates.com

Ordering Information:
Quantity sales. Special discounts are available on quantity purchases by churches, associations, and others. For details, contact the "Special Sales Department" at renewedchristianpublishing.com.

Dear Sisters: Twelve Ways to Grow Authentic Community with Your Sisters in Christ/ Kaye Mayes. -- 1st ed.
ISBN-13:
978-0692887400
ISBN-10:
0692887407

*This book is dedicated to all women who are
yearning to strengthen relationships with their sisters
in Christ.*

For there is no friend like a sister in calm or stormy weather; to cheer one on the tedious way, to fetch one if one goes astray, to lift one if one totters down, to strengthen whilst one stands.

Christina Rossetti

Martha,

May God bless you as you read this book. It is my prayer that He guides you and leads you as you put these steps into action that you may grow closer to Him and to your sisters.

In Him,

Kaye Mayes

Contents

Acknowledgements

I want to thank God first for laying this on my heart to pray about, study, and then to write this book. I thank Him for guidance, endurance, and faith in me, His child.

I want to thank one of my Dear Sisters, Carolyn Hazen, for encouraging me, lifting me up in prayer, and listening to me throughout this entire work.

I want to thank my grandmother, Audrey Brooks, for being so supportive of me throughout my life and especially throughout this process. Thank you to my mother also, who has prayed endlessly about this book from the day I first told her of my plans.

I want to thank my friends and family who have supported me throughout this process and have said uplifting, encouraging words which motivated me to continue this far.

I want to thank the ladies class at the Shelby church of Christ who sat through thirteen weeks of listening to me as I processed what I had studied and tried to teach it as I was writing. They were all so encouraging and patient with me.

I want to thank my REFIT® friends for showing me unconditional love even before God gave me this plan.

I want to thank Matthew Miller, my publisher and editor, for all the guidance and recommendations he has given to help make this book more readable and for his encouragement throughout the publishing process.

I want to also thank my editors for their time and willingness to help make this book readable as well.

Last, but certainly not least, I want to thank my husband and children for their support throughout this process. To my husband, Craig, as he spent so much time managing our money and not allowing me to be discouraged about the costs. As he said, "If this is God's plan, He will see it through to the end." To my children, Sara and Caleb, for their inspiration and encouragement for me to follow through with God's plan.

Preface

Dear Sisters,

The journey of this book began with a heavy heart. I took my heavy heart to God, and He has chosen this as a way to reach out to Christian women, as I feel His heart has been heavy as well. I have felt such disconnect with my sisters for a while and it hurt my soul to see that we have not known each other as well as we should. We are indeed sisters as God has adopted us into His family of believers and we are all siblings, not to be in rivalry, but to work together for the good of our Father to do His will. Who is my sister, I ask? Any woman who is also a child of God; an heir of righteousness through His Son, our Lord and Savior, Jesus Christ. As my sister, I would love to get to know you. Whether we meet personally or not, this book will help us learn how to be Dear Sisters to every sister God puts in our path. Each chapter will address ways we can be a sister to those around us. At the end of each chapter, there is an opportunity to dig deeper into God's word and discuss questions of reflection for every lady who is eager to be a Dear Sister. I challenge you to go through this study as an extra time of meditation and reflection, to help you live out love. Now, let's open our minds and hearts as we strive to be Dear Sisters.

Introduction

My life has changed since December 31, 2013. I started working out with a group of ladies once a week. Not only did my physical life change as I lost weight and toned muscles, but I started seeing changes in my spiritual life. Now, I am not going to say it is all because I started working out weekly. Let me step back and say that God has had this plan for me for a while now. He started revealing Himself long ago, when I was a child and became a Christian. I went to a Christian college and grew on a foundation that my parents, grandparents, and many other church family members instilled in me. Only while at college, the decisions were mine and not my parents'. I grew spiritually, and my confidence in Christ grew as I taught Sunday school and became active in the young-adult class. Then, Satan got hold of me. Not all at once, but little by little, he weaseled his way into my life, leaving me dry and bitter. I slowly let go of my church commitments and my church family. Those were dark days.

But there was one lady in particular whom God worked through. She started slowly slipping God back into my life ever so gently. Then, when I least expected it and thought my life was really going downhill, I saw

His light. I saw it in her. She was there for me in ways she will probably never know. She brought me back to God without even realizing it. She invited me to a youth retreat that her husband was speaking at. Her motive to get me there was to meet his cousin—his single, Christian cousin, who was older and more mature and knew what he wanted in life. I almost refused to go when I realized a man was involved; I was done with men. I did go, for God. I knew my life was going in the wrong direction, and if I wanted to survive here and for eternity, I needed to get my life right with Him. That was twenty-two years ago. Eighteen years later...

An acquaintance invited me to a workout class that she was teaching at her church. I nervously and almost reluctantly went. I did not know anyone there except her and did not know if I would be ridiculed, rejected, or what. I am so glad I went. All the ladies there were so nice. They were encouraging and uplifting. I had fun, lots of fun. I came home so energized and happy that my husband practically pushed me out the door the next Tuesday. Like I said earlier, though, I was changing in more ways than physically and even emotionally.

Let's go to spring 2013, about six to eight months earlier. A sweet lady from church came up to me one day and told me she wished we could have a ladies' retreat. I agreed and went on my merry way. A few months later, another sweet lady came to me. She said the same thing. I agreed and went on my merry way. It was about October or November that I remembered these two incidents. I found it odd that both ladies, not knowing that the other had said or would say anything, had mentioned this to me. I found myself thinking about it more and more. Then, I started praying about it—praying for someone to step up and organize this event, that is.

Then, that day when I went to the workout, I got this feeling that I was the one who should organize the retreat. I love to organize events; why not me? Well, as time went on, I did organize a Ladies' Day. I could not find enough speakers, so I ended up speaking also. God truly blessed me that year. I grew closer to Him and gained self-esteem, becoming more and more physically fit (to do the Lord's work).

Our little workout group grew in 2015. We had more instructors and more opportunities to go work out. I could work out up to three days a week if I wanted to. I quickly realized that it was not just the working out that I really enjoyed. It was the community. The time I had to fellowship with other Christian women in my area.

Then, I grew sadder about the sisters in my own congregation. I was growing so close to other Christians, and that was, and still is, wonderful. I looked forward to each time I could spend with them. I enjoyed encouraging them and being encouraged by them, associating with them and other women in the community who may not be Christians or are weak in their faith, listening to each other, and showing compassion toward one another. But my church family did not feel like family to me. It hurt...really hurt. I really struggled with this. I even thought about going somewhere else to worship. But God intervened once again at just the perfect time. He's so good at that.

I was asked to organize yet another Ladies' Day. Then, I was asked to teach our ladies' class. Let me just say, doing more work is not what gets you closer to God. Sometimes it draws you further away. Or, at least, that is what I have experienced in the past. However, because of struggles and then seeing the need at church, I stuck it out and started praying about it more. I had my good days of focusing on God and my bad days of forgetting about the One who made life possible. We all do at times. It was not until I was at my lowest that I went to Him begging. *Lord, I know I need to focus on You more. What can I do for You?* Quick disclaimer: don't ask that question unless you are serious about it.

So, here I am today. Following God's plan for me. He has asked me to study His word, help others study His word, and reveal to my sisters in Christ just what He wants us to do and how He wants us to live. He gave me the motivation and courage to start studying and writing this book to share with each of you so that our sisterhood will draw us closer to Him and to each other as sisters in Christ.

CHAPTER ONE

Draw Near to God

Worship is the submission of all our nature to God. It is the quickening of conscience by His holiness; the nourishment of mind with His truth; the purifying of imagination by His beauty; the opening of the heart to His love; the surrender of will to His purpose—and all this gathered up in adoration, the most selfless emotion of which our nature is capable.

William Temple[i]

CHAPTER ONE

Draw Near to God

As a young adult, I was a child of God who allowed Satan to slip into my life. I let my work and my non-Christian coworkers and friends sway me away from church and ultimately God. The less time I spent with other Christians, the less time I spent with God. The less time with God, the further I grew away from Him. This caused some dark times in my life. I quit attending church services and participating in activities with the young adults from church. Deep down I knew this was wrong, but I seemed okay with it for a while. It was not until I let go of my relationships with some of the non-Christians I had been involved with that I really saw how dark life had been for me. I had to start somewhere to get my life back with God, and that was by talking to Him in prayer, spending time with Him in His word, and drawing near to Him once again. Do you know your Father? Is it not true that the more time we spend with someone, the better we get to know that person? Why not start with getting to know our Heavenly Father? Ephesians 6:10–20 tells us to "be strong in the Lord and in his mighty power." As we put on the armor of God, we strengthen ourselves against the devil's schemes. Philippians 2:1–11 lays out Christ's attitude and challenges us to have that same attitude. But if we do not spend time with our Heavenly Father and His Son, we cannot be strong in Him or follow His attitude. First, we need to get to know Him better. The best way to do that is to draw near to Him—to read and meditate on His word daily and to talk to Him through prayer. I love what the psalmist said in Psalms 34:8, "Taste and see that the Lord is good; blessed is the man who takes refuge in Him." By drawing near to God, we are seeing His goodness and learning how to give and take in a relationship. This will build a foundation for us to become Dear Sisters.

Exodus 33:18–19 demonstrates a conversation between God and Moses. Moses has drawn near to God and has asked God to help him. He is unsure of his ability but knows that God has the ability to lead the Israelites. "Moses said, 'Now, show me your glory.' And the Lord said, 'I will cause all my goodness to pass in front of you, and I will proclaim my name, the Lord, in your presence. I will have mercy on whom I will have mercy, and I will have compassion on whom I will have compassion.'" God's true glory is found in His character. Moses drew near to God, and he saw God's glory. We can too, if we just draw near to Him.

Another passage that is great for reading as we draw near to God is Ecclesiastes 5:1–7. Here the writer tells us to guard our steps when we go to the house of God. This is not just a meeting place such as a church building; rather, anytime we come to Him in worship (whether public or private), we should "stand in awe of God."

Joshua urged the Israelites to serve the one God. He gave them the choice in Joshua 24, but in verse 15 he says, "But as for me and my household, we will serve the Lord." We, too, have a choice. Thanks to God's grace as His Son died on the cross for us, He does forgive us. However, we never know when we will draw our last breath. Isn't it much sweeter to draw near to Him than to just peer at Him through the window? I am so thankful that God gave me another chance with Him. I am grateful for those who continued to admonish and encourage me as I was led astray, and that I finally realized those dark days would not get any brighter without God at the center of my life. We learn from John about walking in the light in 1 John 1:7 where He instructs us that "if we walk in the light, as he is in the light, we have fellowship with one another, and the blood of Jesus, His Son, purifies us from all sin." We are saved by grace if we have faith. So, with our little "mustard seed" faith (Matt. 17:20), draw near to God, and our faith will grow stronger. This faith is what leads us to want to draw near to Him even more. It is a cycle: God gives us grace because of His love, our belief helps us realize His love and grace even more, and this realization causes us to want to grow our faith in Him. Our faith is strengthened, and we want to share His love with others. Others see His grace and love through us.

Even Jesus drew near to God. In the Garden of Gethsemane, He spent time with His Father. He was sorrowful and troubled. His soul was overwhelmed. We, too, have moments of sorrow and trouble. We, too, feel overwhelmed at times. Jesus did not say, "Wipe away all My tears, Father." He said, "If it is possible, may this cup be taken from me. Yet not as I will, but as you will." *Wow!* He knew He was soon to be put to death, but He was willing to let that happen, knowing that it was His Father's plan (Mark 14:32–42). Do you draw near to God when you are struggling? It seems that we often turn to Him more when we are struggling than when things are going well for us. We feel there is no need to bother Him if all is well. Luke 2 tells us that Anna, after her husband's death, lived in the temple. She never left the temple. She spent each day and night worshipping her Father through fasting and prayer. We see this in Luke 2:38: "She gave thanks to God and spoke about the child to all who were looking forward to the redemption of Jerusalem." So if you are struggling, drawing near to God will help you throughout the process. And if you are not struggling, drawing near to God will help you focus on His glory and see the blessings He has granted you. The psalmist states it well in Psalms 34:5 when he says, "Blessed are those who dwell in your house; they are ever praising you."

The Hebrews writer is calling us to persevere in Hebrews 10:22–25. He tells us that we should draw near to God with sincere hearts. He goes on to say that this happens when we have faith in the One Who cleansed us from guilt and shame. Our sins have been washed away with Christ's blood, and we have been cleansed in the newness of life. Let us choose to draw near to God for this reason, as a thank-you for all He has done for us. We know that there is not enough we can do to pay this debt we owe, but out of our love for Him and our desire to know Him more, we should choose to seek His presence as often as possible. Spend time thanking Him for all He has done for us, asking Him to guide us through our day, seeking His presence in all we do, and so on. Spending time reading His word and meditating on it is another way to draw near to Him—even if we just pick one short passage a day and read it, pray about it, and focus on that thought as we go about our day. Asking ourselves how we can apply that passage to our daily life will help us draw closer to God and His plan for our life. We can even draw nearer to Him through serving others. This will not only help us come closer to God, but it will help us come closer to our brothers and sisters in Christ and to those in our neighborhoods who may not even know God.

Chapter One: Draw Near to God

Discussion

1) What is your favorite setting for drawing near to God?

2) What are some struggles that keep you from spending time in God's Word?

3) What challenges do we, as women, face that leads us to putting God on the "back burner"?

Dig deeper

1) How close do you feel to your Heavenly Father at this moment?

2) Read Hebrews 10:22-23. Write in your words how the Hebrew writer is wanting you to draw near to God.

3) Under the old covenant, God's people could not come near Him to offer their sacrifices of love, and forgiveness without going to the high priests. Today, under the new covenant, we have Jesus Christ as our Mediator. Take some time to read and meditate on this

great blessing with have now. Thank God for His sacrifice and your salvation. Take a moment to read Hebrews 7:11-19 and Hebrews 10:19-25.

Thoughts to ponder

Do you feel the urge to come even closer to your Heavenly Father? What would it mean to you to drink of the "living water" Jesus offered to the lady at the well in John 4?

Diving into action

Spend at least ten minutes each day reading and meditating on God's Word and take time to ask Him what He wants of you (if you are willing to take on His plan).

CHAPTER TWO

Encourage Your Sisters

The Gift of Laughter...Clip cartoons. Share articles and funny stories. Your gift will say, "I love to laugh with you."...The Gift of a Compliment...A simple and sincere, "You look great in red" and "You did a super job" or "That was a wonderful meal" can make someone's day.

Sandi Duncan[ii]

Encourage Your Sisters

Have you ever told a child to do something and he asked, "Why?" One response we tend to give is, "Because I told you so." Children may not understand the big picture like we do as adults. It is the same with our childlike relationship with our Father. He sees the big picture. He knows what will happen if we do not follow His instructions, just as we know that if our small child touches a hot stove, she will get burned. She has not experienced this yet, so she does not know. Well, our Father has told us to encourage one another. So we should do just that. He knows that by encouraging others, we will help them, and that will also bless us. Hebrews 10:24 states, "Let us consider how we may spur one another on toward love and good deeds." One way to do this is to encourage each other. Saying kind and uplifting words is one way to encourage others. Other ways to encourage our sisters may just be to acknowledge their presence and speak to them.

So how should we encourage our sisters daily? Most of us do not see our sisters every day. We see them on Sundays and maybe at a midweek Bible study if they go and we go. What about the sisters who do not go to church regularly? What if we do not go to church regularly? Ephesians 5 starts off telling us to be imitators of Christ. In chapter 1 we discussed one example of Jesus drawing near to God. So we too should draw near to Him if we are going to imitate Christ. Ephesians 5:2 tells us we should live a life of love just as Christ loved us. He even gave His life for us. Should we not give of our time for others? First, I want to encourage us to draw near to God not only in our daily one-on-one time with Him, but also in spending time in worship with a group. As we worship Him, we should be there in fellowship encouraging our sisters. We should allow them to encourage us as well. It will do us all some good.

In the last chapter, I discussed how we should draw near to God in a daily time with Him. I have learned that I have to be intentional about reading God's word. It is like changing our eating lifestyle. We have to be intentional about our eating habits, and we have to be intentional about our spiritual "eating" habits as well. And when we make a mistake and eat unhealthy or skip our study time, it is okay. We are forgiven, and we move forward, striving to be more intentional with our changing habits about drawing nearer to our Heavenly Father. This is the same with encouraging others. Not only do we need to spend more time worshipping with our sisters, we also need to make ourselves available to others to see when and how to encourage them and to allow others to encourage us in our daily lives.

How can we encourage our sisters daily if we do not see them daily? We can call them, write them notes, or send them e-mails or social-media messages. There are so many ways we can connect without being face to face with every sister we know. In Ephesians 4, Paul talks about having unity in the body of Christ and how to live as children of light. As Paul instructed those in Ephesus, we too should live a life of unity. We can do this by living in unity with one another, not talking harshly to others or being inconsiderate of their needs. We should build others up by speaking kindly toward them and showing compassion toward them. Let's get deeper than just calling and writing notes. Let's be intentional about what we say and how we say it. I heard a story of a lady who, without thinking about it, told another lady that she had lost too much weight and should go to the doctor. What she did not know was that the lady had an eating disorder. This comment, as innocent as she may have meant it to be, hurt the lady so much that she quit going to church. There was another time when a lady spoke out in a group setting asking about how to deal with rebellious teenagers. Without thinking or even knowing that the lady was referring to her own family, another lady spoke up and said parents should not wait until their kids are teenagers to worry about their rebellious ways. We really need to think before we speak. Sometimes it is how we say something. Sometimes it is the words we choose. Ask yourself these questions as you think before you speak:

T—is it true?
H—is it helpful?
I—is it inspiring?
N—is it necessary?
K—is it kind?[iii]

By being "imitators of God" and living the "life of love," we are showing others the love that Christ had for us as He "gave himself up for us as a fragrant offering and sacrifice to God" (Eph. 5:1–2). We too should sacrifice ourselves in a way to bring hope to those around us. We can do this by trusting in God to help us share our joy and peace with those around us. "May the God of hope fill you with all joy and peace as you trust in him, so that you may overflow with hope by the power of the Holy Spirit" (Rom. 15:13). This is one of my favorite passages in the Bible. It is because of the hope we have in God that we have joy and peace in our lives. It is also because of this hope that we can share Christ with others and encourage others. Romans 8:9–17 tells us that if we belong to Christ, we have been given the Spirit of God. We have an obligation to live according to the Spirit of God and not a sinful nature. "Now if we are children, then we are heirs—heirs of God and coheirs with Christ, if indeed we share in his sufferings in order that we may also share in his glory" (Rom. 8:17).

In 1 Corinthians 13, we are shown what love is. In verse 4, love is kind. In verse 5, love is not rude or self-seeking. Love is not easily angered. If we are kind, not rude or selfish, and not easily angered, we are showing love to others. We are encouraging, at the surface. Let's take it a step further: not only being kind, but being uplifting. Lift others up with your words and your actions. Have you ever had a time when you wanted someone to just hug you and say, "It will be all right" or "I'm praying for you"? How encouraging it must be to know that you have friends who take time out to (a) notice when we are discouraged or down about something, (b) acknowledge that they notice, and (c) offer to lift us up in prayer to our Heavenly Father.

We will discuss further how we can encourage each other daily in upcoming chapters. Some of these ways are associating with our sisters, spending time with our sisters (outside of worship time), and listening to our sisters.

One Sunday when I was snowed in, I was listening to Dr. Charles Stanley on the television. He was talking about how God encourages us through His word, prayer, friends, and blessings. He asked a great question. How many friends do you have? How many true friends? Friends whom you can call and say, "I need you to come pray with me," and they are with you in no time. Those are true friends. Encouragers from God.

I know you have heard the saying, "It takes a friend to make a friend." Well, this does not apply to us directly, as we are sisters regardless of our view of each other. However, I would say it takes a Dear Sister to make a Dear Sister. Now, let's open our minds and hearts as we strive to be Dear Sisters by encouraging one another in our daily lives.

Chapter Two: Encourage Your Sisters

Discussion

1) Think of your talents and skills. How can you use them to encourage your sisters?

2) When was the last time one of your sisters encouraged you? How did that make you feel?

3) When is the last time you encouraged one of your sisters? How did that make you feel?

Dig deeper

1) Hebrews 10:24 in the Easy-to-Read Version, says that "We should think about each other to see how we can encourage each other to show love and do good works." Write in your words how you can encourage your sisters in Christ.

2) Ask God to show you who needs your encouragement and find ways that she needs to be encouraged. Create opportunities to show her God's love through your words and works.

3) Philemon's love and encouragement to others was an encouragement to Paul. Read Philemon 1:4-7 and meditate on this passage. Ask God to help you be a "Philemon" to those around you.

Thoughts to ponder

Do you feel God's encouragement even when you have been hit hard and feeling low? Take Eliphaz's words to heart as he spoke to Job when he was feeling low and hit hard. Read Job 4:1-6. Let God be your hope in the tough times. Even when you feel nobody on earth is encouraging, allow God to be your encouragement.

Diving into action

Think of some ladies you have missed seeing in Bible class or group study lately. Spend time in prayer for each lady and then find ways to encourage her. Maybe she is just discouraged and needs a little boost to remind her that we are all in this life together and you are there to help her through this rough spot.

CHAPTER THREE

Associate with Your Sisters

Surround yourself with good people. Whether they're the best or not, people are capable of learning if they've got good hearts and they're good souls.

Kid Rock[iv]

CHAPTER THREE

Associate with Your Sisters

I have a friend named Wanda. We originally met several years ago at our family dentist office where she works. She and I have since connected in a workout community called REFIT®. We have enjoyed spending time together talking about our concerns for others and how we can let Jesus's light shine through our lives. One night while we were talking, she told me this story and has since given me permission to use it.

Sitting in church one Sunday I heard a lady ask, "What's your name?" I replied, "Wanda." A few minutes later this same lady, who had Parkinson's disease and several other debilitating diseases, asked again, "What did you say your name is?" I replied again, "Wanda." A few minutes later, with a look of concern the lady asked a third time, "Could you please just tell me your name one more time?" As I turned around that third time to look at her and reply, I felt as if God himself were sitting there saying, "Are you who you say you are?" I then replied, "My name is Wanda Jones. It is so nice to meet you, Sandy."

Wanda told me the lady did not make it back to church many more times before her health worsened. But Wanda learned so much from Sandy asking her not once but three times who she was. It reminds me of when Jesus questioned Peter three times, asking him if he loved Him. Do we love Jesus? Do we love Him enough to feed His sheep?

In John 10, Jesus says that He is the Shepherd, and He tends to His sheep. But in John 21, Jesus appears to his disciples a third time after being raised from the dead. In verses 15 through 19, Jesus asks Peter, "Simon son of John, do you truly love me more than these?" Peter says, "Yes, Lord. You know that I love you." Jesus says, "Feed my lambs." Once again Jesus asks, "Simon son of John, do you truly love me?" Peter answers, "Yes, Lord, you know that I love you." For the third time, Jesus says to him, "Simon son of John, do you love me?" Hurting, Peter says, "Lord, you know all things; you know that I love you." Jesus replies, "Feed my sheep..." Do we feed God's sheep? I know we are not one of Jesus's original disciples as Peter was, but we are still called to help each other out, to keep one another from falling in the pits of sin and the valleys of spiritual comas. We are called to hold each other accountable. How can we do that if we don't even talk to our sisters? Just as we have to draw near to God to get to know Him, we must associate with our sisters to get to know them, to know each other's strengths and weaknesses.

We need to be willing to associate with all of our sisters, no matter the race, color, financial background, or past they have led, as we are told in Romans 12:16. Can you imagine if you were the sinful woman told about in John 8 and none of your sisters would associate with you? Can you imagine being one of the accusers of her sins who brought her to Jesus? We are all sinners. Christ paid the debt for all of us. God gives us all grace. Does this give us the right to only associate with whom we want to? Remember the Samaritan woman whom Jesus spoke to at the well in John 4? The custom back then was for men to not associate with women. It was also custom for Jews to not associate with non-Jews, especially Samaritans. Yet Jesus spoke to her anyway. He even told her about the "living water" that He could give her. Had Jesus not associated with this woman, neither she nor many other Samaritans would have come to know Jesus and believe Him. By associating with our sisters, we are opening doors for a disciple relationship that may just grow her faith as well as ours. We are called to love one another, and what better way to show our love for our sisters than to associate with them?

Just imagine, had the lame man's friends not carried him to the house where Jesus was speaking and opened a hole in the roof and let him down to Jesus, he would not have heard Jesus speak, and more so, he would not have been healed in front of so many witnesses. I know what you are thinking. *Well, I have kids to raise,* or *I have aging parents to take care of. I don't have time to deal with someone else's muck and issues in life. I have enough of my own.* Remember Judas? Jesus associated with him just as He did with his closest friends and disciples. Yes, He spent more time with them than with Judas. He enjoyed their time together. But when it came down to it, He also associated with Judas. In John 13:1–30, Jesus knew that Judas would betray Him, and yet He still invited him to the Last Supper. Not only did He extend an invitation to dinner, He also washed Judas's feet along with the other disciples' feet. This is a great passage to focus on, as it can move us deeper into the heart of God and the love of Jesus. John 13:34–35 tells us, "A new command I give you: Love one another. As I have loved you, so you must love one another. By this all men will know that you are my disciples, if you love one another."

Another lesson learned from Wanda's story brings up this question: Are we who God wants us to be? Are we the same person at church, at the grocery store, at home? Are we genuine children of God? Wanda had the opportunity to visit with Sandy while she was in the hospital not long before she died. Wanda made sure to tell Sandy just what an impact she had made on her. Do we tell others when they affect our lives for the good? Do we watch for ways God can use us and listen when He gives us instruction? Do we thank Him and those He puts in our lives and allow them to work in us for good? Wanda encouraged Sandy and her family not only by visiting her that day, but by expressing her gratitude for Sandy.

A lesson I learned the hard way about associating with others happened about twelve years ago. There were two different ladies who attended church where I did. They each had a small child and were pregnant at the time. Both of them had husbands who worked on the weekends a lot, leaving them to get themselves ready, get a child ready, and get to church to worship with a young child all alone. I had young children at the time myself. But I had a husband and a mother-in-law there to help. We sat up front, and these ladies sat in the back. I would see them when I had to take my children out on occasion. I would speak or wave and move on. One day I noticed that Jessica was no longer coming. Before I knew it, Rebecca quit coming as well. I met with Jessica in her home one day after she had quit coming to our church. She told me what it felt like to be a "single mom" at church with a young one. She said she just could not take it anymore. She said, "Yeah, people spoke and were courteous, but that was about it." See, our congregation was small, and while we had a nice room for a nursery, it was not staffed. And while our congregation had some really friendly people, they were not quite as helpful as they could have been. Jessica helped me understand that it is not all about saying, "Hi, how are you?" It is deeper than that. We must be willing to go the extra mile. Reach out to one another and offer a helping hand. Offer to meet with someone outside of church services.

I reconnected with Rebecca when my son went to preschool. She had started attending the church that my son's preschool was at, and her son was in another class there. We would see each other in the hall waiting to pick our sons up. Rebecca and I started talking, and she expressed some of the same feelings Jessica had. Rebecca actually had her second child while still attending with us, but she had a very hard time managing to get herself, a toddler, and a newborn up and ready by herself and make it to services. When she did manage to do it, she was exhausted by having to manage feeding the newborn and disciplining the restless toddler. She was getting nothing out of the services. So she chose to go somewhere where there was a staffed nursery and women willing to help her out. It saddened my heart to know that I was so wrapped up in my own life that I missed opportunities to reach out and associate with these ladies.

Do you get to Bible class or worship service just in time to sit and worship? Do you leave as soon as the last "amen" is said? Consider spending a little more time in fellowship either before or after services, associating with your sisters and brothers in Christ. We need to associate with our sisters not only before and after church services, but throughout the week as well. Some great ways to do this are by speaking to them if we see them in the grocery store, calling and inviting them to coffee or a walk, or even visiting them throughout the week. I have a sister who became discouraged after having surgery and not being able to attend services for a few weeks while she was recovering. She said nobody had called to check on her or to offer the Lord's Supper to her while she was not at church. We all need to be observant to others' needs and share our love with our sisters by associating with them. We like it when others spend time with us, so we should look for ways to spend time with others. God is the same in that He wants us to spend time with Him. He enjoys talking to us and listening to us. Spending time in prayer each day is a great way to show compassion to Him and to one another.

Chapter Three: Associate with Your Sisters

Discussion

1) Discuss a time when you struggled with associating with a sister in Christ? (no names please)

2) How can we express our gratitude to those who have impacted our lives?

3) What talents or circumstances has God given you that can be used in associating with your sisters?

Dig deeper

1) Read John 13 and ask yourself, "If I were Judas, would I want Jesus to treat me the same as the others around the table?" Now ask yourself, do I treat others as God treats me?

2) While spending quiet time with God, ask Him to show you someone to associate with. Ask Him to help you during your time with this person that you may shine His light and love to her.

3) In II Timothy 1:16 Paul recalled Onesiphorus coming to see him while in prison. Onesiphorus' asso-

ciation with Paul refreshed Paul's spirit. He was not ashamed that Paul was in prison. Let Onesiphorus be an example to you and an encouragement to you as you associate with your sisters.

Thoughts to ponder

In Romans 12:16, Paul is telling us to be "willing to associate with people of low position." Who do you know that is not in the same social status, financial bracket, or class of intellect as you? Do you spend time with that person?

Diving into action

Think of a sister you do not know well and seek to meet her. Plan to get together with her and get to know her. Associate with at least one sister (or more if God sends more your way).

CHAPTER FOUR

Refresh Your Spirit of Compassion

The gift of Affection...Be generous with appropriate hugs, kisses, pats on the back and hand-hold. Let these small actions demonstrate the love you have for family and friends...The gift of Cheerful Disposition...The easiest way to feel good is to extend a kind word to someone. It's not that hard to say "hello" or "thank you."

Sandi Duncan[v]

CHAPTER FOUR

Refresh Your Spirit of Compassion

Imagine coming inside to grab a refreshing glass of cold, sweet lemonade after being out in the hot summer sun. Now, imagine if that glass was actually a glass of lemon juice. Did your lips pucker up? Mine did, just thinking about it. Lemon juice has that effect on us. But lemonade, on the other hand, is quite refreshing, especially on a hot summer afternoon. What is the difference? The sweetness of the lemonade makes it refreshing. We too can live a life of bitterness, or we can add sweetness to our life and be refreshing to those around us.

Psalms 103:6–10 reveals God's compassion toward His people. David, the psalmist, is referencing God's compassion shown toward His people in Exodus. We see the Lord's compassion and grace when we study Exodus 32–34. Remember when God instructed Moses to write the laws and commands on the tablets of stone that He provided (Exod. 24)? The next several chapters give detail on more instructions given to Moses while he was on Mount Sinai with God. At the end of chapter 31, the Lord tells Moses to instruct His people to observe the Sabbaths as a sign between God and His people for generations to come that they may know that "I am the Lord who makes you holy" (verse 13). "When the Lord finished speaking to Moses on Mount Sinai, he gave him the two tablets of the Testimony, the tablets of stone inscribed by the finger of God" (verse 18). In the meantime, the Israelites had convinced Aaron to make an idol to worship. God became so angry because of this lack of obedience and respect from His people that He wanted to destroy them. Instead Moses sought the favor of the Lord and reminded God of His promise to Abraham, Isaac, and Israel that their "descendants would be as numerous as the stars in the sky."[vi] Then Moses, in his anger toward the people, broke the stone tablets, and he took the golden calf idol and melted the gold and ground it into powder, scattered it in the water, and made the Israelites drink it. In chapter 34, God instructed Moses to chisel out the laws and commands on a new set of stone tablets. Rather than being bitter, the Lord had compassion for His people. In Exodus 34:5–7, we see that the Lord is the Lord of compassion and grace. He is patient, loving, faithful, and forgiving. This does not mean that the guilty go unpunished, but it does mean that God loves us enough to be patient with our mistakes and is willing to forgive us. This is most apparent in the life of Jesus Christ and the ultimate display of forgiveness as God in the flesh suffered and died on the cross to save each one of us. Jesus's compassion was displayed numerous times throughout the New Testament as well. For example, in Mark 6:33–34, Jesus had been with the apostles and gathered around many people for a while and had not even had a chance to eat. They decided to go to a quiet place to eat and get some rest. They got in a boat, but many people saw where they were headed and ran on foot to beat them there. They wanted to be with Jesus. In verse 34, Jesus's compassion compelled him to begin teaching them. And they did get to eat, thanks to the compassion of a boy sharing his lunch and God making sure there was enough for all.

Psalms 118:24 tells us, "This is the day the Lord has made; let us rejoice and be glad in it." Further down in verse 29, the psalmist says, "Give thanks to the Lord, for he is good; his love endures forever." Do we rejoice in the daily blessings God shares with us? Are we thankful for God's goodness and love? I'm sure those people gathered around Jesus were thankful for His teachings and the food that was shared that day. When we are thankful, we add sweetness to our life, and in turn we become more compassionate toward God and others. Do you know anyone who is thankful for everything? If so, have you noticed what a blessing that person is? Have you noticed that person probably has a lot of friends? We like to be with positive, loving, grateful people. It helps us to be that way as well. Romans 12:10 instructs us, "Be devoted to one another in brotherly love. Honor one another above yourselves." Romans 13:8–10 tells us that if we love our neighbor as ourselves, we are fulfilling the law. I remember as a child learning the meaning of the acronym JOY: Jesus first, others second, yourself last. This is what the first and second commandments are all about. Love God, and love your neighbor (Matt. 22:37–39).

In 2 Corinthians 1, Paul told the church in Corinth that God is "the Father of compassion and the God of all comfort." He comforts us in our troubles so that we can comfort those around us. Two chapters ago we talked about encouraging our sisters, and I mentioned being imitators of God. Ephesians 4:32–5:2 gives us an example of how we can imitate God. We are instructed to "be compassionate to one another, forgiving each other, just as in Christ God forgave you." So, just as God comforts us in our troubles, we can comfort others with our compassion and kindness for them. We can not only refresh our spirit of compassion, but we can also refresh others' spirits by adding sweetness to their lives through love.

Throughout the Bible we are instructed to love others. 1 Corinthians 13 is the go-to passage telling us what love is. In 1 Peter 3:8, Peter says, "Finally, all of you, live in harmony with one another; be sympathetic, love as [sisters], be compassionate and humble." Colossians 3:12–17 gives us more instructions on how we can live as holy and dearly loved, chosen people: "Clothe yourselves with compassion, kindness, humility, gentleness, and patience." I am reminded also of the fruit of the Spirit in Galatians 5: "But the fruit of the Spirit is love, joy, peace, forbearance, kindness, goodness, faithfulness, gentleness, and self-control." And in Philippians 4, we are told that "whatever is true, whatever is noble, whatever is right, whatever is pure, whatever is lovely, whatever is admirable—if anything is excellent or praiseworthy—think on such things." Paul goes on to say in verse 9, "Whatever you have learned or received or heard from me, or seen in me— put it into practice. And the God of peace will be with you." We should not look at all these passages as to-do lists or read them and think, *I could never do all of that.* While we are told that we must love one another (John 13:34–35), God did give us the freedom of choice. We have the choice to follow these instructions and live a full life or to follow our own wishes and see what happens in life. However, I feel that if we draw near to Him and feel His presence, we will have the desire to at least strive to follow these guidelines. Not as rules and must-dos, but simply as a guide to get us through life and closer to Him.

Remember in the last chapter about Jesus asking Peter to "feed my sheep" (John 21:17)? In Luke 15 Jesus tells a parable about lost sheep. After reading Luke 15:1–7, think about all the sheep God has sent your way. At a recent Ladies' Day our church had, one of the speakers spent time with us going through Psalm

23. Not just reading it, but looking at it in a shepherd's perspective. One point she made has stuck with me ever since. She said that sheep who stay nearest each other and the shepherd are guarded the most. That makes sense. We are God's sheep. He is our Shepherd. Those of us who stay nearest to each other and our Shepherd are the most protected. Through this parable, I feel like Jesus is saying, "Hey, I won't be here on earth to protect My sheep, so you all need to huddle around each other and encourage each other to stay near the Father and the other sheep so you are all protected. Oh, and if one sheep does go missing, help Me look for her, and when she does come back to the fold, we all need to jump up and down for joy and show our love to her."

Dear [sisters], let us love one another, for love comes from God. Everyone who loves has been born of God and knows God. Whoever does not love does not know God, because God is love. This is how God showed his love among us: He sent his one and only Son into the world that we might live through him. This is love: not that we loved God, but that he loved us and sent his Son as an atoning sacrifice for our sins. Dear [sisters], since God so loved us, we also ought to love one another. No one has ever seen God; but if we love one another, God lives in us and his love is made complete in us. We know that we live in him and he in us, because he has given us of his Spirit.[vii]

I reviewed this passage with a third-through-fifth-grade class recently. One of my students said he has a hard time loving a certain person. We had a good discussion about how we really do not know God if we cannot find a way to love everyone. This comes easier for some people. Some people are loveable, and then there are others whom we struggle with loving. We do not have to agree with their lifestyle or their decisions. We need to learn to love them as God loves them and loves us. God looks past our flaws and sees us as His creation, and He loves us for who we are. That does not mean He is pleased with our lifestyle choices or the decisions we make. One way we can practice this unconditional love is by being sincere with ourselves and with those around us. By genuinely loving someone, we are showing God's love to others, and we are showing God that we can love others with *agape* love.

Chapter Four: Refresh Your Spirit of Compassion

Discussion

1)   After reading John 13:34—35 discuss how others can recognize the love you have for them. How can you recognize the love your sisters have for you?

2)   Today is the day the LORD has made. How can you rejoice and be glad in it?

3)   Tell about a time when a sister refreshed your spirit of compassion. What did she do that made you feel loved?

Dig deeper

1)   Read I John 4:7—13. Meditate on this passage.

2)   While spending quiet time with God, ask Him to refresh your spirit of compassion so that you may continue to love others as He has loved you.

3)   I John 3:24 states: "How do we know that God lives in us? We know because of the Spirit he gave us." (ERV) Thank God for the Holy Spirit dwelling in your

heart. Be refreshed and show others how they too can have the Spirit living in them.

Thoughts to ponder

Do you show others grace and compassion as God has over the years? Read Nehemiah 9:26—31. God never walked away from His people for good. He truly is the God of grace and compassion. We too should continue to show compassion toward our sisters. But we cannot do this alone. We need God at the center of our hearts, reminding us of His ultimate example of love and grace to refresh our hearts.

Diving into action

Refresh your spirit of compassion by looking for a wayward sister and encouraging her. Refresh her with your love and kindness.

Sincerity of the Heart

Only those who have learned the power of sincere and selfless contribution experience life's deepest joy: true fulfillment.

Tony Robbins[viii]

CHAPTER FIVE

Sincerity of the Heart

As you have been reading, you can see that each chapter is building on the last. Being a Dear Sister takes time, patience, love, and attention toward God and others. It also takes a heart of truth. When we work on all these aspects in our walk with God, we will not only draw closer to our Father but also draw closer to each other and bring others closer to Him in the meantime. This cannot be done as a checklist though. It must be done with a sincere heart, one that is willing to change, willing to grow.

Romans 12:9 tells us, "Love must be sincere," but what does it mean to be sincere? *Sincere* means "free of dissimulation (honest); free from adulteration (pure); marked by genuineness (true)."[ix] The Greek word ἀνυπόκριτος (an/upo/kritos) means "genuine, sincere" or literally in this context "without hypocrisy."[x] The Latin derivative of the word *sincere* is "clear/unclouded; free from fever; pure with no admixture of foreign material."[xi] So Paul is telling us that we should have a pure, honest, true love for others. It should be clear of any foreign materials such as greed or selfishness. As sisters we need to encourage each other with a genuine, loving attitude. We can do this by associating with one another because we truly love each other. We should be honest with ourselves, God, and our sisters as we reach in toward our hearts, reach up to God, and reach out to one another. Keeping God at the center of our lives will help us all be more sincere. Paul is a great example of loving without hypocrisy, as he wrote in 2 Corinthians 6:3–13. He is telling those in Corinth about his hardships and how those hardships have helped him be a better servant of God. In verses 6 and 7, he states that it was not only his hard work, suffering, sleepless nights, and hunger that helped him, but it was his "purity, understanding, patience and kindness; in the Holy Spirit and in sincere love; in truthful speech and in the power of God." If we read further in verses 11 to 13, we see that Paul and his companions reached out to the Corinthians with sincere hearts, and they asked that to be done in return to them. We all need sincere love in our lives. This helps us truly know that the other person is honest and genuine and is not hypocritical toward us.

In 1 Peter 2:1, Peter is telling us as Christians that we should get rid of all malice, deceit, hypocrisy, envy, and slander. As we get rid of these contaminations, we need to fill the holes in our lives with what is right. Ephesians 4:20–5:21 is full of ways we can fill our lives with purity leaving behind the foreign materials of contamination. I encourage you to sit down and read this passage as a whole and meditate on it. For now, we will break it down and study parts of it. First Paul tells us to "put off your old self" in verse 22. He does not stop there. In verses 23 and 24, he says we should "be made new in the attitude of your minds; and to put on the new self, created to be like God in true righteousness and holiness." How do we do this? In verse 25, he says to "put off falsehood and speak truthfully" to our neighbor. Paul breaks it down a little for us in the following verses as he tells us not to sin because of our anger, not to go to bed angry, not to give the devil a foothold, not to steal, to work with our own hands to share with others, not to use unwholesome words in our conversations, not to grieve the Holy Spirit, and to get rid of bitterness, rage and anger, brawling and slander, and every form of malice. Instead, we should build others up in the way we talk to them. Be kind and compassionate to everyone, forgive each other, be imitators of God, and live a life of love as Christ loved us. Paul goes on in chapter 5 to tell us of more impurities we should get out of our lives. By encouraging others, being kind and loving toward everyone, forgiving each other, and imitating Christ's example of selfless love, we can have a sincere heart, one that is full of love and not hypocrisy.

Hebrews 10:22 states, "Let us draw near to God with a sincere heart in full assurance of faith, having our hearts sprinkled to cleanse us from a guilty conscience and having our bodies washed with pure water." A sincere heart begins with baptism, that pure water of Jesus's sacrifice. We accept His sacrifice to give us a new life that is pure, and it continues with faith in Him and acting in love.

In 1 Timothy 1:3–5, Paul says that the goal of the command of God "is love, which comes from a pure heart and a good conscience and a sincere faith." Paul is talking to Timothy and warning him about false teachers. False teachers do not teach out of love or from pure hearts. They do not use a good conscience or have sincere faith. God commands us to love. He wants us to speak the truth to those around us. He also wants us to do so with a sincere heart. How can we have love and a sincere faith? With our actions. In 1 John 3:18, the writer tells us we should love not with words, but with actions and in truth. I can't help but think of my children when they were younger and would fuss with each other about little things. Of course, to them at the moment, it was huge. We would tell them to apologize to each other. They would take turns facing each other but looking down and mumbling, "I'm sorry," in the most insincere tone possible. But I knew they really meant it when I looked in the room to see them sharing and talking to each other nicely again. I look back now and wonder if I did the right thing by making them say their apologies. Was that teaching them to be sincere? Speaking in truth may be sincere, but acting in truth and honesty shows sincerity to those around us even more clearly.

Honey made by bees is pure. Unfortunately, as with many products, manufacturers have ways of adulterating the honey by diluting it in order to make more money. I found some ways of checking for the purity of the honey: (1) know your region's honey purity laws; (2) check the label, but don't take it for granted; and (3) taste the honey if a sample is offered.[xii] Let's look at this in relation to us as Christians: (1) know God's laws (1 Tim. 4:11–16); (2) look at ourselves and really examine our minds (Phil. 4:8); and (3) "taste and see that the Lord is good" (Ps. 34:8). By reading and understanding God's word and examining our own lives, we are able to better discern if we are living a life of sincerity—one that is true to ourselves, God, and others.

Paul talks in 2 Corinthians 4 about pottery. He compares us to jars of clay. God is the potter, and we are the lump of clay. He takes His time forming us into what He wants us to be shaped like. As you know, pottery starts out as a piece of clay, but once shaped, it is heated at high temperatures to keep that shape, to mold it. This heat leads to a permanent change as it increases the strength of the clay, and it hardens and sets its shape. Before the piece of clay can be shaped, it must be prepared. Paul tells the Christians in Corinth that they were "hard pressed on every side, but not crushed; perplexed, but not in despair; persecuted, but not abandoned; struck down, but not destroyed." He continued to tell them that we carry Jesus's death around so that His life would be revealed in us. Jesus's death on the cross was the ultimate sacrifice, and yet that self-sacrificing love has made us whole and full of life. Further down in the chapter, we read, "All this is for your benefit, so that the grace that is reaching more and more people may cause thanksgiving to overflow to the glory of God." God's grace for us should not stop with us. We should share this greatest love with those around us. In 2 Corinthians 4:18, Paul says, "So we fix our eyes not on what is seen, but on what is unseen. For what is seen is temporary, but what is unseen is eternal." If we focus on God and His unfailing love for us and not on all the trials in our life, we will be better able to show sincere love to those around us. Once this piece of clay is formed into a masterpiece by none other than our Creator, He uses us to share His love with those around us and bring Him the glory of His artwork.

My daughter made a piece of artwork in her art class at school. It was a gingerbread house made of clay. It had windows in it. I asked her if I could take it to my ladies' class to show them, since we were talking about pottery. She told me not to forget the light. I was not planning to bring the light as I did not think it related, but while reading 2 Corinthians 4 again, I was amazed at what I read. Just as this clay house has holes in it for the windows, we too have holes in our lives. God put those holes in our lives so that His light might shine through for others to see (2 Cor. 4:4–6). Those holes in our lives are made from high temperatures. Some of us need more heat than others to make more holes and shape us just right to share our lives with others. While we tend to think of these holes as upsets in life such as sin, sickness, and trials of many kinds, God is using each of these to strengthen us and mold us. Then, when He is ready, He allows His light to shine through us to others so that they may better see Him living in us and around us.

James tells us to "consider it pure joy" when we are under the heat of life. God has taken us, a lump of clay, and worked on us to shape us. Then, we undergo the heat of trials. This is the testing of our faith to see if we can hold that shape, to strengthen our lives. James 1:12 tells us, "Blessed is the |woman| who perseveres under trial, because when [she] has stood the test, [she] will receive the crown of life that God has promised to those who love him."

An example of women with sincere hearts of love and faith is found in 2 Timothy 1, where Paul recalls the sincere faith of Timothy's grandmother and mother as they raised him. And because of the way they led their lives full of sincerity, this character was carried on to Timothy. What a great legacy we can leave when our children and grandchildren see our honest, pure, true life of love and faith, and hopefully they choose to follow it as well. Remember that as we come closer to God, encourage others, and associate with others, all with sincere hearts, we are reaching out and showing God's love to those around us. We are letting our lights shine as Jesus has instructed.

Luke 10:38–42 portrays an example of two women, friends of Jesus. Both had sincere hearts. Martha opened her home up to Jesus and his disciples. She was so eager to prepare them a meal. She worked hard at this, but she was upset that her sister, Mary, was fixated on Jesus as she sat at his feet and listened to him. Both ladies were loved by their friend Jesus. Both of them were sincere in their love for Jesus. But Jesus did say that Mary had chosen the better thing to focus on. It was not that Jesus did not want Martha to open her home or to prepare a meal. It was that she was "distracted by all the preparations" (verse 40). She was so focused on making the food perfect that she neglected the time she had to spend with Jesus and listen to him. Sometimes we as women get so wrapped up in the material things of life or on checking off our to-do lists that we forget to stop and focus on God and other people; we forget to focus on the important things in life, such as pure hearts, true love, and honesty. We may be so busy feeding the hungry that we forget to speak to them. We may be so busy stuffing shoe boxes that we forget to pray for the children around the world who need to hear God's word. We may be so busy praying for the sick that we forget to go visit them. "Love is primarily giving. It's an action that leads to a feeling, not a feeling first."[xiii] Let us show our love sincerely toward God and others.

Paul and Timothy's prayer for the church at Philippi was "that your love may abound more and more in knowledge and depth of insight, so that you may be able to discern what is best and may be pure and blameless until the day of Christ" (Phil. 1:9–10). This is my prayer for each of us as well. That we may all grow closer to Christ in our study and understanding and that we may be able to better understand what is pure and blameless and then follow that.

Chapter Five: Sincerity of the Heart

Discussion

1) What does a sincere heart look like to you?

2) Are you ever "distracted by all the preparations"? (Luke 10:38—42)

3) How can women be less distracted with our daily lives so we can have a true heart for God and our sisters?

Dig deeper

1) Read Acts 2. This is a great example of community that we have been given from the early Christians. Not only did they eat together and open their homes up to one another, they did so with gladness and sincere hearts. Look for opportunities to open your home up to others and then pray that God opens your heart and your desire to really "want" to do this. Be happy about the time you spend with them.

2) In I Peter 1:22, Peter had been talking to the Christians about being holy. He writes: "Now that you have purified yourselves by obeying the truth so that you have sincere love for each other, love one another deeply, from the heart." We have been instructed to

love one another deeply, from the heart—that is having sincerity of the heart.

3) While spending quiet time with God, ask Him to give you opportunities to have a sincere heart to those around you.

Thoughts to ponder

What are some ways that you practice real love? I John 3:18—20 in the Message translation reads: "My dear children, let's not just talk about love; let's practice real love. This is the only way we'll know we're living truly, living in God's reality. It's also the way to shut down debilitating self-criticism, even when there is something to it. For God is greater than our worried hearts and knows more about us than we do ourselves." I want to encourage us all to go out and practice real love. Show others the love of God that dwells in your heart. Be a light to others. As Jesus says in Matthew 5:8: "Blessed are the pure in heart, for they will see God."

Diving into action

Work toward building a better relationship, a sincere one, with a sister you have not already connected to. Remember to be pure, true, and honest. Be full of grace and love.

CHAPTER SIX

Intimacy with God

The Gift of Solitude...There are times when we want nothing better than to be left alone. Be sensitive to those times and give the gift of solitude to others.

Sandi Duncan[xiv]

CHAPTER SIX

Intimacy with God

"Be still, and know that I am God" (Ps. 46:10). What does this mean to you? Do you ever stop? I don't mean sitting on the couch watching a Hallmark movie. I mean focusing on God—the Father, the Spirit, and the Son. Talking to God and then just listening for His reply. I feel like this is the topic I struggle with the most in this book. I have a hard time stopping and focusing only on Him. I am sure I am not alone in this. Women are multitaskers by nature. That in itself is enough to cause us to have a hard time putting everything down and spending all of that allotted time focusing on one thing. Add to that our duties as wife and mother and employee (if we work outside the home), and we have a busy schedule. It takes a lot of self-discipline to put our main focus on what is unseen when we see that the laundry is knee deep, the kids are hungry, our husband just walked in the door...and the list goes on.

I had the opportunity to go on a retreat a while back. I had just come out of a bad relationship and, I will admit, not one willed by God. The lady who invited me to the retreat wanted to introduce me to her husband's cousin who was planning to be at the retreat as well. "He's a nice man, a godly Christian man. You need to meet him," Lynette said. I told her I was not going to meet another man. I was done with men; however, I realized I needed to reacquaint myself with God. That weekend, I spent a lot of time sitting still and listening. We were staying near a nature trail and waterfall. This was a great opportunity for me to get out into God's nature and spend time with Him, praising Him and admiring His creation. I did meet the godly Christian man, and God did bring us together a little later. More importantly, that weekend retreat was time for God to change me. Then, after my heart was changed, He worked to get us together. I am happy to say that we have been married for twenty-one years now and grow closer to each other and to God each year. I would go as far as to say that the more time we spend with each other, the more intimately our lives are intertwined. We understand each other more now than we did even five years ago.

It is the same with God. The more time we spend with Him, the more intimate our moments together become. The more time I spend with God, the more I understand Him, and the more time I want to spend with Him. We will never fully understand His deep love for us and how much He wants us to love others as

He has loved us, but we do gain a little more of an understanding each time we listen and become intimate with Him. Our intimacy with Him also teaches us how to be intimate with those He puts in our lives.

I believe the more time spent with God, the more we see what His plans are for us. Intimacy is more than just drawing near to God. It is the next step to a deeper relationship with Him. Intimacy is a close familiarity or friendship. It is not one sided. When we draw near to God, we are learning more about Him. But when we become intimate with Him, we are opening ourselves up completely to Him without fear or reservation. I think of Enoch in Genesis 5:22–24. There is not much said about him except his age and that he "walked with God." He walked with God for 365 years, and then God took Enoch to be with Him forever. They must have been close, intimate friends for God to want to take him from this earth to be with Him at that time. Of course, we do not know details or reasons. Maybe it is just me speculating.

Elijah is another man who was intimate with God. In 1 Kings we see how Elijah worked hard for God. In chapter 19 we read that Elijah was afraid and ran for his life. He ran into the wilderness and sat down and prayed to God before falling asleep under a bush. "I have had enough, take my life; I am no better than my ancestors" (verse 4). God sent an angel to wake him up, and He provided food for Elijah. After being strengthened from the food, he traveled on for forty days and nights, and then he came to a cave and went inside it to spend the night. While he was in the cave, the word of the Lord came to him and asked what he was doing. Elijah talked to God and expressed his frustrations and loneliness. God then instructed him to stand on the mountain in the presence of the Lord as He passed by. Great winds came, an earthquake came, a fire came from the earthquake, but God was not in any of those great, powerful moments. It was in a gentle whisper, which came after all of this, that Elijah heard the Lord's voice speaking to him. God asked Elijah why he was there in the cave. He then listened to Elijah. After listening to Elijah, the Lord offered him guidance. Do you ever feel like you are the only one teaching a Bible class, hosting youth events, or organizing church activities? You are not alone. Elijah felt this way as well. But because of his intimate time with God, he was able to get the help, strength, and encouragement he needed. There may be times in our life when we feel God's presence, but many times it takes us being still and listening for His gentle whisper to really know what He is telling us.

Elijah's intimacy with God not only helped him, but others saw this close relationship and wanted to have that as well. In 1 Kings 19, God had instructed Elijah to anoint Elisha to succeed him as prophet. Elisha went with Elijah without reservation. In 2 Kings 2:1–11, we see that the time had come for Elisha to take over Elijah's job as prophet. These men had spent time together getting to know one another, and Elijah had taught Elisha all he knew about prophesying for God.

Three times Elijah tried to leave Elisha so God could take him without Elisha watching. And three times Elisha refused to let him out of his sight. In verse 9, Elijah asked Elisha if there was anything he could do for Elisha before he was taken from him. Elisha replied, "Let me inherit a double portion of your spirit." See, even Elisha saw how close and intimate Elijah was with God, and he wanted that too. Do those living around you know that you are intimate with God? If we listen for His guidance; if we allow Him to walk with us through our troubles, heartbreaks, and fears; if we talk to Him and listen to Him, then we have an intimate relationship with Him. We become so close that we eventually let go of those fears.

I think of Jesus and how He knew that He would be crucified, but when troubled about it, He went to His Father and talked to Him. Overwhelmed and sorrowful, He prayed to God. He accepted God's will to be done, and in Luke's account in 22:43, an angel appeared to Him and strengthened Him. God knew His Son needed strength to get through this, because They had an intimate relationship. Intimacy is not one sided. We must be excited about loving our Lord. We must focus on our relationship with Him. We must recognize and acknowledge His blessings. Mostly though, we must know that this relationship with Him is unconditional. He loves us regardless of our scars, faults, and fears. His love is not judgmental.

There are several others in the Bible who had an intimate relationship with God. I think of Abraham, who became the father of many nations; and Moses, who met with God on Mount Sinai to receive the Ten Commandments and came down from the mountain glowing from being in God's presence. And what about David, a man after God's own heart? And I think of Paul, who was once a persecutor of Christians and was blinded by God and turned his life around so much that he prayed and sang praises to God within that nasty inner cell chamber. He spent his new life sharing God's love with so many others and setting the example of how to walk with God through his daily life. I think of Anna, who spent the end of her life in the temple worshipping God daily. I think of Mary and Martha, who spent time with Jesus while He was here in the flesh, and they became close friends. And what about John, who in Revelation 1:10–11 said, "On the Lord's Day I was in the Spirit, and I heard behind me a loud voice like a trumpet, which said: 'Write on a scroll what you see and send it to the seven churches.'" I don't think God would pick John as the one to record his sightings from this experience and send it out to the seven churches if they did not have an intimate relationship.

Not only do we need to draw near to God and study His word, we need to become His friend. How do we do that? I would suggest that we spend time with Him, walk with Him, have confidence in Him, and share an affection with Him. Don't be afraid to talk to God with your deepest thoughts. He already knows what is in your heart and on your mind. So you might as well share it with Him. Then, listen to His gentle whisper as He protects you, provides for you, and guides you. Maybe keep a diary of your walk with Him so that you can go back and review to see where you were, see where you have come, and maybe even add goals to see where to go next in your relationship with Him. I know this seems nearly impossible for the young mom or the working woman or even the widow who just lost the love of her life. But this is an important part of our Christian walk. It may sound ritualistic, but maybe those with time restraints could work this into their calendars. Kind of like a young married couple with small children scheduling a date night. I laugh when I think of my husband and me as we created "date nights" as our children became old enough to stay at home alone for short periods of time. We would ride together to fill up our vehicles' gas tanks. We still do this today. That is time for just the two of us. While it may just be thirty minutes away from the kids, we know that we can talk about issues or just be with each other without our children's ears and mouths. Maybe we, as women, need to make excuses to get alone with God more to fill our "love" tanks with our Heavenly Father. He is ready to listen to us whenever we are ready to confide in Him.

Chapter Six: Intimacy with God

Discussion

1)   What does Psalm 46:10 look like to you? Describe a setting that helps you have an intimate time with God.

2)   Name a person in the Bible who inspires you to become more intimate with God. Why?

3)   Why is it so hard for us, as women, to stop and focus on the One who loves us the most?

Dig deeper

1)   In John 14:6, Jesus tells his disciples that "I am the way and the truth and the life. No one comes to the Father except through me." Further down in the chapter Jesus says he will ask the Father to send the "Spirit of truth" (or Holy Spirit) to those who know him. Today, those of us who believe Jesus is our Lord and Savior have the Holy Spirit living in us. The Holy Spirit is our guide, intercessor, and encourager. The Holy Spirit will teach us and remind us of what we have already been taught. This should give us peace and keep fear from our hearts. When we become intimate with God, we feel the Holy Spirit alive and well within our hearts.

2) In Psalm 9 we read how David gives thanks and sings praises to God. He knows that God reigns forever. He knows that God is his refuge and a stronghold in times of trouble. Read verse 10. Do you know God? Do you trust in Him? Do you seek Him? Spend time in meditation about this verse. Seek God. Sing praises to Him. Give Him the glory for all the blessings you have received. Put your complete trust in Him.

3) When times were tough, David went to God. Read Psalm 69. Go to God in your troubled times. Seek His favor. He is ready and waiting for you to call out for help. "[Y]ou who seek God, may your hearts live!" (v.32b)

Thoughts to ponder

Whether we are having good days or bad days, God wants to be near us. He wants us to come to Him whether to give Him praises and glory or to seek His guidance and protection. I am reminded of Paul and how he praised God even in his troubled times. Read Acts 16:16-28. While Paul and Silas were in prison, they had some intimate time with God. Through their singing praises and praying, other prisoners heard them. Then, they all had a chance to escape the prison bars when an earthquake shook the prison doors open and their chains fell off. But, they all stayed put. Let us all remember to stay put, sing praises to God and seek His protection even when we feel imprisoned in the fear and trials of life.

Diving into action

Find a few minutes to spend alone with God. Carve out time on your calendar if need be. Find a quiet place. Take your Bible, a devotional book, journal book or diary, and a pen. Spend time as God's friend. Adore Him and all He has blessed you with.

CHAPTER SEVEN

Sounding Board: Listen to Your Sisters

To listen is to love, and you can't love unless you listen.
And Christians are often not very good listeners. We're too
busy preaching and correcting and judging.
Preston Sprinkle

The Gift of listening...but you must really listen. No
interrupting, no daydreaming, no planning your response.
Just listening.
Sandi Duncan[xv]

Sounding Board: Listen to Your Sisters

Proverbs 18:13 reminds us that as we are listening, we should do just that. We don't just stand there thinking of the next thing to say or even answer the other person as he or she is still talking. I don't know about you, but this is one area of my life that I am constantly working to improve. I come from a talkative family, so it is hard for us to stop and listen to someone else without wanting to interject our two cents' worth. In Proverbs 17:27, the writer tells us, "A man of knowledge uses words with restraint." We are to simply listen. Be a sounding board. Sometimes all it takes is a listening ear. We need to be one who does not speak up and try to solve problems or one who does not spread the news to all around as a gossip; rather, we need to be one who just listens. When we are asked to give advice, we need to seek

God's wisdom and guidance so we are not just giving our opinion. James 1:19 puts it like this: "My dear [sisters], take note of this: Everyone should be quick to listen, slow to speak and slow to become angry." We have been instructed as God's children to listen to one another. Proverbs 21:13 warns us of what happens to those who do not listen to others: "If a [woman] shuts [her] ears to the cry of the poor, [she] too will cry out and not be answered." In Psalms 34:15, David said that God's eyes are on the righteous, and his ears are attentive to their cry. We should follow God's ways. Let's be attentive to our sister's cry! Women need someone to talk to in confidence, knowing their thoughts will not go anywhere else. When our sister comes to us about something on her heart, we need to be attentive to this and listen without spreading her words to others.

Proverbs 11:13 warns us that those who gossip betray confidence. Do you feel like you can confide in someone who gossips to you? I know I don't. It makes me wonder if she is telling others what I may have confided in her about. Proverbs 16:28 warns us that a gossip separates close friends. To have close friends, we need to be trustworthy in our friendship. I like the Message translation of Proverbs 18:8. It says, "Listening to gossip is like eating cheap candy; do you really want junk like that in your belly?" When we eat candy, we enjoy it as we chew on it, but then we regret the added fat and calories we indulged in. This is how gossip is. We enjoy hearing the "juicy news," but then once we have heard it, we regret that we wasted our time listening to it and that we have this information in our minds that we do not need. We are not following God's will, and we are hurting ourselves as well as those we gossip about, not to mention the risk of hurting those who hear the gossip as they are tempted to keep spreading such nonsense. Proverbs 26:20 warns us again about gossips. The writer relates a gossip to a fire: "Without wood a fire goes out; without a gossip a quarrel dies down." So we should not only listen to our sisters, we should do so carefully so as to not listen to gossip and especially not spread that gossip on to others.

Paul tells the church at Ephesus in Ephesians 4:29 that they should not let any "unwholesome talk" come out of their mouths. They should build one another up "that it may benefit those who listen." The Easy-to-Read version puts it this way: "When you talk, don't say anything bad. But say the good things that people need—whatever will help them grow stronger. Then what you say will be a blessing to those who hear you." We too should follow this advice. When a sister is listening to us, we should talk to her in a way that builds her up. We need to think about the impact our comments will make on her. If we are not building her up, we may just tear her completely down. By saying good things, we will be a blessing to those listening to us.

I have a few friends, sisters in Christ, whom I know I can reach out to, and I know they will listen to me and will not spread the information to others. They will build me up when I am discouraged. Sometimes I seek advice, and they give it. Sometimes I just want someone to listen to me as I vent my frustrations or think through something out loud. Is that not what God asks of us? To be there for each other to comfort, encourage, and exhort one another? How can we do this if we do not listen to one another? How can we do this if we do not allow others to listen to us?

In Acts 10:22–26, we see that Peter met with Cornelius at his house. Cornelius and his family and friends listened to Peter. Of course, Peter reminded them that he was only a man himself when they bowed down to worship him. While it is good to have friends to talk to us about our spiritual life, we need to remember that they too are human. While we should be there for each other, God is our ultimate source of encouragement and guidance. Sometimes this is hard for young women who see a more mature woman who appears to have a perfect life. We want to do just as she has done, thinking it will make our lives perfect also. This is not the case. While the more mature woman talks to the younger woman, she should explain what she went through in life to get to where she is now and that life is not perfect without God at the center, and we should worship Him and no human.

In 2 Corinthians 6 and 7, Paul talked to the church at Corinth about his hardships. He wanted them to listen to what he had to say for several reasons. He wanted them to see his struggles, where he had been, and how he got to the place he was now, so they could see that life is not always easy. He wanted them to listen to him so they could learn how to be better Christians. By listening to him, they became more serious. They wanted to prove they were not in the wrong. They wanted to see Paul and make sure the right things were done. By listening to each other, we can learn from our sisters how to become better children of God. We can grow closer to each other in a serious relationship. By listening to a more mature sister, we can gain a better understanding of how to see God's plan for us. By listening to a younger sister, we can better see the need she has to grow closer to God. This will help us as we exhort our sisters. We too should want to be helped by those God puts in our lives to mentor us. In 2 Corinthians 7:4, we see that Paul was encouraged. He was comforted by Titus's coming and that the Christians were concerned for him. Had Paul not listened to Titus or Titus to the church, they would not know of the concern and would not have been encouraged or comforted. Further down in chapter 7, Paul exhorted the Christians in Corinth through a letter. He spoke to them, and they listened. He knew they listened because they were sorry for some things that had happened that led up to the letter, and they repented of their wrongdoing. We will talk more about this in a future chapter, but I wanted you to see how important it is that we as Christians should consider spending time together, listening, and talking about our walk with God.

We are one in Christ, and we need to remember that without hope of eternity and without God as our source of salvation, we are separate from Christ and our sisters. In Ephesians 2:13–22, we see that Christ is the chief cornerstone that joins us together and "in him you too are being built together to become a dwelling in which God lives by his Spirit." I believe Colossians 3:12–17 sums it up well for us:

Therefore as God's chosen people, holy and dearly loved, clothe yourselves with compassion, kindness, humility, gentleness, and patience. Bear with each other and forgive whatever grievances you may have against one another. Forgive as the Lord forgives you. And over all these virtues put on love, which binds them all together in perfect unity. Let the peace of Christ rule in your hearts, since as members of one body you were called to peace. And be thankful. Let the word of Christ dwell in you richly as you teach and admonish one another with all wisdom, and as you sing hymns and spiritual songs with gratitude in your hearts to God. And whatever you do, whether in word or deed, do it all in the name of the Lord Jesus, giving thanks to God the Father through him.

In this passage we have an outline for how we should live our lives and the way we should treat those around us. Why? Because we were called to peace. When we listen to our sisters with a heart of love, kindness, humility, gentleness, and patience, when we forgive our sisters and love each other, the peace of Christ will dwell within our hearts.

Now is a good time to start practicing this yourself by finding some sisters who will listen to you and allow you to listen to them. You may be wondering where to start. I suggest praying to God and asking Him to guide you to a sister you can listen to or one who will listen to you. One-on-one meetings with a sister or small-group studies are helpful for opening up. I went through a small-group book study recently and enjoyed getting to know some of my sisters more as we opened up to one another about various topics. By attending a weekly ladies' Bible class, you can get to know some sisters a little better also. As an extrovert, I don't find it hard to open up to others, but introverted ladies may find it somewhat overwhelming to speak out in class. One suggestion could be to start out by offering to read scriptures when prompted. These are not your words, thoughts, or views, so it may not seem like you are opening up at the time. As you attend and speak out more through reading, you will hopefully gain trust in the other ladies, and you will feel more comfortable opening up to them with your words, thoughts, or views. If you are a leader of a ladies' group, put yourself in your group's shoes. Make sure the discussions do not become gossip sessions. Do not force ladies to speak out, but welcome any discussion that comes (as long as it is not gossip). Remember to greet your newcomers or those who do not attend regularly. Have a brief introduction time so ladies can introduce themselves, and allow newcomers the opportunity to introduce themselves as well. If you are part of a ladies' group, leader or not, make sure you are trustworthy. What is said in the group time stays within that group. Speaking freely of a confidential conversation causes trust to fall by the wayside, so that ladies no longer feel comfortable opening up. If you are new to a group, speak when spoken to, introduce yourself, and keep an open mind, even if you have had a bad experience with another group of women. Be sure not to judge the new group based on your past experience. If you are not already part of a Christian community such as this, I want to encourage you to look for one. Reach out to a friend whom you already confide in and see if she is part of a group that you could go to with her. Being open in a group setting is not something that will happen overnight. It takes encouragement, associations, and compassion toward someone for her to know she can trust you. Draw near to God, become His intimate friend, and your sisters will see this and want to become intimate friends with you as well. And you will want to become intimate friends with them as you reach out and love each other. The more time you spend with your sisters, the more opportunities you will have to open up and listen to one another.

Chapter Seven: Sounding Board—Listen to Your Sisters

Discussion

1) Why should we be quick to listen, slow to speak, and slow to become angry? (James 1:19)

2) How can we gain trust in our sisters so they will be more open with us and allow us to listen to them?

3) Often it takes us getting out of our comfort zone to become better listeners or to be able to open up to our sisters. Think of a time you have had an opportunity to step out of your comfort zone to listen more or to open more. Did you take this opportunity? Why or why not?

Dig deeper

1) Read Psalm 31 in the Message Bible. While this is mostly about David talking to God and expecting God to listen to him, there is mention of gossips in this passage as well. Think about chapter 6 (Intimacy with God) and this chapter as you meditate on the words of the Psalmist. Talk to God about your struggles. Tell Him all your troubles knowing that He is listening to you and He will guide you. Listen for His gentle whis-

per. Then, study on the negative effects gossip had on David (see verses 13, 18, 20). Remember this in your daily life and avoid gossip-filled conversations.

2)   Not only should we not be part of gossip, we also need to think before we speak and make sure we are not speaking to someone harshly or wishing evil upon them. Read the following passages and ask yourself before talking to your sisters: "Do I speak to my sisters in a way that is uplifting and edifying or do I speak harshly and with ill-intent?" Read Psalm 41:4—7; Ephesians 5:4—7; I Timothy 1:5—7.

3)   Paul warns Timothy about young widows spending their time in gossip in I Timothy 5:11-15. I believe this goes for any woman young or old, married or not. This is a temptation for all of us. We must heed these warnings of listening without spreading gossip. Be prayerful about how you act and react when a sister talks to you in confidence. Listen! If she requests advice, give it out of love and with God's guidance! Do not tell others of your conversation!

Thoughts to ponder

"To listen is to love, and you can't love unless you listen. And Christians are often not very good listeners.

We're too busy preaching and correcting and judging." What does this quote mean to you? Do you love your sisters? Do you listen to your sisters without preaching, correcting, judging? There is a time and place to talk to our sisters in love about their spiritual issues, but there are times when we just need to shut out mouths and open our ears and listen to what they have to say.

Even if you are a young lady, you can still be an example to your sisters. 1 Timothy 4:12 states that: "You are young, but don't let anyone treat you as if you are not important. Be an example to show the believers how they should live. Show them by what you say, by the way you live, by your love, by your faith, and by your pure life." (ERV)

Diving into action

Reach out to a sister and let her know you are willing to listen to her if she needs to talk. Be a sounding board for her, but remember this should be done in confidence.

<u>CHAPTER EIGHT</u>

Togetherness:
Get Out and Do Things
with Your Sisters

Coming together is a beginning; keeping together is progress;
working together is success.
Henry Ford[xvi]

CHAPTER EIGHT

Togetherness:
Get Out and Do Things
with Your Sisters

A community, as defined in the dictionary, is "a unified body of individuals; a group linked by a common policy."[xvii] Are you part of a community, in particular a Christian community? The last chapter challenged us to listen to each other. We can certainly "listen" to others via social-media messages, e-mails, texts, and phone calls. But isn't it better to be face to face with our sister so she can see our concern and see that we are truly listening? When we come together, we can hug our sister and tell her we love her even through the muck in her life. In this chapter we will focus on spending time together with our sisters, one on one and as a group. The more time we spend with each other, the more we get to know one another. This leads to building great relationships. In Romans 15, Paul encouraged the Christians in Rome to be strong for the weak, build each other up, come together in unity for Christ, and glorify God. In verse 13 he says, "May the God of hope fill you with all joy and peace as you trust in him, so that you may overflow with hope by the power of the Holy Spirit." When we spend time with others, our hope should overflow to them. If we don't spend time with our sisters, how can they see the overflow of our hope? This hope spreads joy and peace to those around us. When we spend time with others, the Holy Spirit is working in us to spread this hope, to encourage our sisters, to build them up, to be united, and to glorify God. Acts 2:42–47 discusses how the early Christians spent time together. They were together daily. Their new life as Christians had them so excited that they wanted to share it with each other and with those they knew outside their new faith. This created a ripple effect, and we see at the end of verse 47 that the Lord added to their number daily. Their hope was overflowing. Is your hope overflowing? Are you spreading joy and peace to those around you?

When we come together with a sister one on one, we have the opportunity to build a friendship. We are able to get to know each another as we listen and encourage one another. When sisters meet together as a group, we build a bond with others so that we may be in unity, and this brings God the glory while also strengthening the weak and humbling the participants.

Paul instructs us in Romans 12:10–16 to be devoted to one another in sisterly love, to share with God's people who are in need and practice hospitality, to rejoice and mourn with those who are rejoicing and mourning, and to live in harmony with one another. How can we do all this if we do not spend time together, getting to know one another and sharing our life with each other? In Ephesians 4, Paul is talking about unity in the body of Christ. He urges us as Christians to be "humble, gentle, patient, bearing with one another in love." He encourages us to make every effort to live in unity with each other. In verse 16 he states, "From him the whole body, joined and held together by every supporting ligament, grows and builds itself up in love, as each part does its work." This passage reminds me of Aaron and Hur as they held Moses's hands up to keep the staff raised as Joshua fought the Amalekites in Exodus 17. Whenever Moses's hands lowered, the Amalekites started winning. So when his hands grew tired, Aaron and Hur would raise them up and hold them there. How can we know when our sisters are growing weak and tired? By spending time with one another, we are able to strengthen the weak and build each other up. We also have the opportunity to see and hear the needs of our sisters.

Jesus showed His love while on this earth by spending time with those around Him. Yes, many were tax collectors and pagans, but He also spent time with His disciples. He even brought three of them with him to the Garden of Gethsemane (Matt. 26:36–46; Mark

14:32–42). This was a time when He was suffering greatly. Jesus knew the time had come that He would soon be leaving this earthly life. He wanted to be with them while He was suffering. He wanted them to see His needs. In Matthew 26:38 Jesus told Peter, James, and John, "My soul is overwhelmed with sorrow to the point of death." He did not tell them so they could fix His problem. He told them so they could better understand His pain. He wanted them to be in His presence. He wanted them to be strong for Him. There is something about having someone by our side when we are troubled. While we are together we can encourage, listen, and have sincere hearts. Jesus also took His disciples with Him as He traveled. In Luke 10, we see that He and His disciples spent time with Mary and Martha. In John 11, after Jesus heard of the plot to kill Him, He decided not to be out in public around the Jews; rather, He went to the village of Ephraim and spent some private time with His disciples. Six days before the Passover, He decided to go spend some time with His friends Lazarus, Mary, and Martha. They held a dinner in His honor. Mary even anointed Jesus with expensive perfume. Jesus knew He would not have much more time to spend with His friends and disciples, but they may not have known. We too do not know when our last opportunity will be to spend time with our sisters. That is why it is important that each chance we get, we should spend time together to encourage one another, listen to each other, exhort one another, and worship with each other.

Paul followed Jesus's lead by spending time with his brothers and sisters when he could. He would much rather have spent time with his fellow Christians in person than write them letters. In 2 Corinthians 12:14–21, Paul wanted to spend time with the Christians in Corinth. It was not because he wanted anything from them, but he wanted to bless them, encourage them, and exhort them. He visited them when he could to encourage them, teach them, and show God's love to them as Jesus Himself did. When we spend time with our sisters, we should also show our love to each other through encouragement, compassion, and exhortation. In Romans 1:8–13, Paul wrote to the Roman Christians stating his longing to spend time with them. He wanted to spend time with them so he could strengthen their faith even more, so that he could encourage them and they could encourage him, and so he could see the good results of his love and efforts as he did from the Gentile Christians. And in 1 Thessalonians 2:1–15, Paul spent time with the church in Thessalonica. During this time he was not only preaching to the Christians there in Thessalonica, he was also encouraging, comforting, and exhorting them (verse 12). By spending time with our sisters, we too can encourage and comfort one another. As we share our struggles and heartaches like Jesus did in the Garden of Gethsemane, as we share our love for one another like Mary and Martha did when they got to spend time with Jesus, and as we listen to what is going on in each other's lives like Paul did when he visited with various Christians during his missionary journeys, we are growing closer to each other as Dear Sisters. In 1 Thessalonians 5:14–15, Paul urges the Christians to exhort, encourage, strengthen, and be patient with everyone. Let us hold fast to God's word and remember to always encourage our sisters, practice hospitality, and be humble, gentle, and patient with one another. Paul knew the depth of togetherness. Do we understand the depth of togetherness?

As a young adult, I made some poor choices in life and chose not to go to church or spend time with other Christian young adults. After pulling away from my Christian community altogether, I started realizing that this was not what God intended for me. I needed encouragement from other Christians. It became a dark time in my life. It was then that I realized why God meant for us to come together regularly. This dark place in my life was not what I wanted or needed, but I was too ashamed and embarrassed to reach out to my Christian community. It was not until I stopped spending time with my non-Christian friends and began focusing on God and asking for His forgiveness that I started rebuilding those relationships that I had lost. Now, I am not saying we should never spend time with non-Christians. How would we share God's love and allow God to work through us to plant that seed if we were never around those in the dark? We need to find the right balance, but we need to keep our focus on God more than anything. When we build the right relationships with other Christians, we are helping each other grow closer to God. It is so important that when we are spending time together, we are encouraging, associating, being compassionate, listening, and exhorting one another. If we are not, we are just being friends who happen to be children of God. We are not being disciples of Jesus, unifying the body of Christ.

In Hebrews 10:25, the writer of Hebrews says, "Let us not give up meeting together, as some are in the habit of doing, but let us encourage one another—and all the more as you see the Day approaching." While we need to meet together at church services, we also need to meet together outside of worship services. When was the last time you spent time with a sister outside of worship services, deepening your relationship? How did it make you feel? I spent time with a friend recently, and it made me feel loved. It also allowed me time to practice my listening skills. It was encouraging for us both to step out of our routine and just get away for a few hours. We talked, laughed, and prayed together. Being in a relaxed setting like this can be a great opportunity to talk to your sister about your struggles and her struggles and to look to each other for exhortation and guidance. This builds you both up and strengthens you as you see you are not alone in life's challenges.

Chapter Eight: Togetherness—Get Out and Do Things with Your Sisters

Discussion

1) How often do you schedule time to get together with other Christian women outside of worship time?

2) Think of a time you spent with a sister. How did you feel before you got together? How did you feel after the time together? Did you gain anything from that experience?

3) Why do you think Paul wanted to visit the churches he had started while on his missionary journeys rather than just writing letters?

Dig deeper

1) John 11:1—44 is the story of Jesus raising Lazarus from the dead. Read this entire passage and then go back and read verses 31—36 again and meditate on it. Put yourself in Mary's shoes. She just lost her brother and feels helpless and hopeless because her friend, The Teacher (Jesus), had not come and healed Lazarus while he was still alive. Imagine how comforting it was for her to have Christian friends gathered around her,

hugging her, praying with and for her, and then following her as she left to make sure she would be okay.

2) Read Acts 16:13—15. This passage is brief but says so much. Lydia was not only a business woman, but she also spent time in prayer with other women. This Sabbath day was special. Paul and Timothy happened to come to the place these women were gathered and talked to them about the Good News. Her heart was open to what these men said and she decided to be baptized. What do you think would have happened had she decided not to get together with these women and pray and fellowship?

3) Read Ruth 1:6—17; 4:13—17. If you are not familiar with this story, I suggest reading the entire book of Ruth (it is only 4 chapters). Ruth stayed with Naomi through thick and thin. They traveled together to Judah. Naomi mentored Ruth in many ways. Then in chapter 4, we see Ruth married into Naomi's family line and through her new husband, Boaz, they had a baby boy named Obed. Obed was the grandfather of David and David was an ancestor of Jesus. These ladies encouraged one another and built each other up even with an age gap. Do you have an older sister who is a spiritual mother to you? Now is the time to get together with one and grow closer to each other and God.

Thoughts to ponder

In Luke 10:38, we see that Martha opened her home up to Jesus and his disciples and there is no mention in this passage that they were friends. Go ahead, read it again! We see later in the gospels that Jesus loved Lazarus, Martha, and Mary (John 11—12), but not at this time. This may have possibly been the first time they met face to face. This is part of togetherness-being hospitable. Think of someone you can open your home up to and in time become a friend.

Diving into action

Spend time with a sister or group of sisters. Plan an outing with sisters in your area. Go to a local coffee shop, go shopping at a local mall, enjoy time together over a meal, go walking together and spend time talking and visiting. Get out and do things together.

CHAPTER NINE

Exhort Your Sisters

Let the gentle bush dig its root deep and spread upward to
split one boulder.
Carl Sandburg[xviii]

CHAPTER NINE

Exhort Your Sisters

As I look back on the dark days of my young-adult life, I recall several meaningful Christian friends trying to stay in touch with me. One friend even offered me a part-time job to keep me occupied and away from my non-Christian boyfriend. Of course, I needed the extra money, so I took the job offer as a means to pay bills. I really enjoyed the time I spent with Bonnie, and that led me to spending more time with my friend Lynette (who was eager to find me a Christian man later on). If it were not for Bonnie and Lynette trying their best to shine God's light on me, I would not be writing this book now. I would likely not be attending church or having anything to do with Christians or Christ. I am so thankful for these ladies and so many others who influenced me for the better without even realizing it. Imagine though if more of my sisters in Christ had taken the time to love on me even before I had quit attending church and young-adult group activities. Maybe I would not have even quit spending time with them. I am not saying they are to blame. I am merely saying I might not have been so easily swayed to the devil's schemes if I had felt more "at home" with my church family. In this chapter I hope to help us all find a way not only to encourage our sisters, but to give each other counsel, to advise each other, and to admonish one another in a way that will strengthen our faith in God and our love for Christ.

As we listen to one another and spend time together, growing closer to one another and loving one another, bearing with one another in love, we are better able to exhort one another. This is not the same as judging others. One who judges another is one who "is authorized to hear and decide on cases, is appointed to decide in a matter at issue; is qualified to pass a critical judgment."[xix] We are not called to judge others' spiritual lives; this is God's authority only. However, we are called to exhort one another by simply helping one another improve without being critical or deciding another's outcome in life.

One example in the New Testament of a sister exhorting a fellow Christian was when Priscilla and Aquila met Apollos. Acts 18:24–26 tells of the account: "When Priscilla and Aquila heard Apollos, they invited him to their home and explained to him the way of God more adequately" (verse 26). Priscilla and Aquila merely explained right from wrong. They advised or counseled Apollos. They did not criticize him or judge him.

In Hebrews 10:24, the writer tells us that we should "spur one another on toward love and good deeds." We, as Christians, are instructed to help each other love others better and do more good deeds—not because this is what gets us to heaven or makes God happy, but because by doing so, we are showing God's love to others so that they may want to know Him and accept His grace. We are letting His light reflect in our lives, and we are becoming the salt of the earth. I know this book focuses on relationships with other Christian women; however, not all Christians are strong or mature. We need to let His light shine in our lives toward fellow Christians just as much as we should toward unbelievers. For we do not want our sisters to fall away from Christ forever. According to Hebrews 6:4–6, it is impossible for those who have fallen away to be brought back to repentance. Not that God will not accept them, but "because to their loss they are crucifying the Son of God all over again and subjecting him to public disgrace." This passage warns us that even Christians can become so hardhearted that they fall from the faith. And that is worse than not becoming a Christian in the first place. We don't want to become like this, and we don't want our sisters to become this way either. That is why we should work with each other to keep our hearts softened to the love of Christ. If you know of a sister in need of a softened heart, pray for her. Then go to her with a loving heart, and talk to her with God's wisdom. Remember to do this confidentially. If going to your sister does not help and you feel you need guidance, go to a trusted leader in your local church, or seek some advice from someone you can trust to help and not hurt the situation.

In 2 Timothy 4, Paul told Timothy that he should "correct, rebuke, and encourage—with great patience and careful instruction." We too should exhort our sisters with patience and love. We should remember to do so with God's guidance and instructions. We must keep the faith and exhort our sisters to do the same. In 1 Corinthians 16:13–14, we are told to be on our guard, to stand firm in our faith, to be women of courage, and to be strong. And to do it all in love. Paul goes on to say in verses 15–18 that he wanted the other Christians to do as Stephanas, Fortunatus, and Achaicus. He said that they "refreshed my spirit and yours also. Such men deserve recognition." They refreshed Paul's spirit by devoting themselves to the service of the saints. Paul was exhorting the Christians at Corinth by advising them of ways they could be better servants of God. Do you devote yourself to the service of your sisters? We should also refresh our sisters' spirits. If we see a sister straying from God's word, we should gently, lovingly, patiently show her how to get back on track again. If we are a sister straying from God's word, we should accept the exhortation of our fellow sisters, as they are just trying to help us improve our walk with Christ.

Paul, Silas, and Timothy exhorted the Christians in Thessalonica as they urged them to "live lives worthy of God, who calls you into his kingdom and glory" (1 Thess. 2:12). Paul was not being judgmental or critical.

He simply encouraged the Thessalonian Christians to live as they knew they should be. Throughout the books of 1 and 2 Thessalonians, we read of Paul encouraging the Christians of Thessalonica and thanking them for their continued love and encouragement for him and his companions. He goes on to remind them to follow God's teachings and not false teachers and to continue to love one another, and then in 2 Thessalonians 3, he points out some issues that he had heard some of the Christians there were struggling with. Paul is a great example of what exhorting versus judging others means. He even explains God's judgment plans to them. This was important for them to understand, as they were Gentiles who were recently converted to Christianity. These Thessalonians were concerned about dying before Christ's return and did not understand God's plan for their eternal life. We too should reach out to our sisters in a loving way to encourage one another and explain God's word to those who do not understand as much. If we do not feel like we can teach them properly, we should find someone stronger in the faith who is willing to help them understand better. As we all face trials and persecutions of a sort, it is vital that we understand God's word and are ready to teach one another as needed. "All Scripture is given by God. And all Scripture is useful for teaching and for showing people what is wrong in their lives. It is useful for correcting faults and teaching the right way to live."[xx]

You may be asking how you can exhort your sister properly. In Galatians 6:1–10, Paul is talking to the Christians in Galatia about exhorting their brothers and sisters. If you are a stronger Christian and you know of one who is spiritually weaker, you should restore her gently. Carry her burdens. We must be cautious though, as we may also be tempted to slip in our faith. We must not have the "better than thou" attitude. We are deceived when we think we are better than others. We should test our actions before becoming proud of ourselves. We cannot compare ourselves to somebody else. We will reap what we sow. A selfish attitude causes us to reap destruction. We need to think about our sister's soul above our desires. Are we focusing on God's guidance to help her, or are we focusing on ourselves (for example, what makes us look good, what is convenient for our time schedule, and so on)? By being selfless, we will please the Spirit and will reap eternal life. We do not want to give up on her. We will reap a good harvest in God's perfect time. Verse 10 tells us, "Therefore, as we have opportunity, let us do good to all people, especially to those who belong to the family of believers."

Heavenly Father, I come to You asking that You open our hearts up. Show us Your mercies that are new every morning. Open our eyes to the needs of our Dear Sisters. Open our hearts to Your love. Open our ears to Your word. Help us see a glimpse of what You see. Show us who to encourage, how to be Your light, and where to be the salt of the earth. Thank You for Your never-ending love and Your heavenly grace. In Jesus's name, amen!

Chapter Nine: Exhort Your Sisters

Discussion

1)   Think about when you were first introduced to Christianity (whether as a child or adult). Who did you talk to about God and His way of living?

2)   Discuss ways we can reach out to our sisters who may need gentle advising.

3)   Why do you feel it is so important for us to listen to a sister's counsel? If you feel it is not important, why not?

Dig deeper

1)   Read Exodus 18:1—27. This story is about Moses talking to his father-in-law, Jethro. Jethro listened as Moses told of all he was doing to lead the Israelites. Jethro was concerned for his son-in-law. So, he counseled Moses on how to lead such a large group. Think of a way you can counsel a younger or less mature Christian woman. Pray for God to guide you in this journey and then reach out to her, helping her in a situation she may or may not realize she is struggling in.

2) Read John 8:1—11. Jesus did not say much to this woman. He did not have to. He was gentle with her and that is what counted the most. She felt His love and concern for her well-being. We too should remember it is not the words we say while counseling others, it is our attitude that means all the world to the receiver of the advice.

3) Read John 4:1—42. Jesus not only spoke to the Samaritan woman at the well. He had compassion on her and He exhorted her. Because of this time of counsel, she believed in Him and ran to tell everyone in town. They chose to come see for themselves, after hearing her testimony, and heard Jesus and chose to believe. Sometimes we do not receive counsel from our sisters. We receive it from God's Word and then we are to share that with those around us. If you need some advice, talk to God and listen through the study of His Word. He will guide you to someone to give more Godly counsel if you ask. He is preparing someone now just for you.

Thoughts to ponder

The book of Proverbs is full of wisdom. Just a few passages in Proverbs about listening to the advice of others include: Proverbs 4:1—2-listening to parental teachings; pay attention; remember what you are taught. This is especially important for children to understand and to follow. Proverbs 13:10-listening to the advice of others will bring wisdom, but those who are proud and argue with the advisor, will not be wise. Proverbs 15:22-ask for advice. Sometimes you must look for others who are wiser and more experienced in a situation and ask them for advice. Proverbs 19:20-listen to the advice given to you and accept discipline. By listening to others who have "been there, done that", you will gain wisdom. It is kind of like learning a lesson from someone else's mistake. Another passage to leave you with is Colossians 3:16 which states:

"Let the teaching of Christ live inside you richly. Use all wisdom to teach and counsel each other. Sing psalms, hymns, and spiritual songs with thankfulness in your hearts to God." (ERV)

Our ultimate Counselor, Advisor, Exhorter should be God, the Father, the Son, and the Holy Spirit. Please know though, that God uses His people to help each other through the tough times, whether it be through listening, encouraging, spending time together, or exhorting one another.

Diving into action

Do you know a sister who is slipping from the faith? Go to God for His guidance and instruction. Draw near to Him, then with listening ears, a sincere heart and a spirit of compassion; go to her. Encourage her as you associate with her and spend time with her. Exhort her in a loving way, giving counsel to her and yet not being critical of her.

CHAPTER TEN

Reverence for God

Pursue some path, however narrow and crooked, in which
you can walk with love and reverence.
Henry David Thoreau[xxi]

Reverence for God

D o you have a dad whom you looked up to as a child? Maybe you thought he "hung the moon." When I was a young child, my dad was an alcoholic. I did not look up to him. I rarely even saw him or knew him. But once he decided to change the path his life was taking, he made a big change. He packed up his family and moved us from south Florida to North Carolina where he and my mom knew one couple. This man and his wife were like parents to my dad when, several years earlier, he was in the navy and stationed in Norfolk, Virginia. They had stayed in touch and encouraged my dad to make the move. My parents, without jobs in North Carolina, decided to take a leap of faith and make the move. My dad quickly found a job and made good friends who were supportive of his new lifestyle and were not bad influences on him. Many of them were from church. I quickly grew fond of this new man he had become. He had always been a hard worker but was not a family man. He would stay out late after work and many times would not get home until after my bedtime. When he was home, he was irritable and cranky. Looking back, I am guessing that was because he did not drink at home, and his body was aching for another drink. So this new life he started leading brought him home after work to spend time with his family.

My dad loved to be outdoors. He would take me fishing at a local lake or river. Sometimes we would go hiking in the backyard. As I got older, he taught me all about cars. He was a shade-tree mechanic. I learned how to change a tire, check the oil and filter, and do so many more things that I cannot remember today. He grew a garden. He loved vegetables, and he loved sharing them with others. I learned a lot about generosity from my earthly father. When he was no longer able to work and was dying of cancer, I saw what bothered him the most. He could not do for others. He could not provide for his family financially; he could not take care of the car or drive it. He could not take care of the yard or his little garden. This hurt him. He felt so unneeded and unappreciated.

I tell you this story to relate it to our Heavenly Father. He is our Sovereign Lord, Creator of all living things. He created us in His image. He even knows how many hairs are on our heads. So why is it that we find ourselves not appreciating all He has done for us and blessed us with? I imagine it hurts Him when we do not appreciate His generosity. In Psalms 33, the psalmist describes just what God has done for us and reminds us that we should praise Him for that. He reminds us in verse 4 that the word of the Lord is right and true and that He is faithful in all He does. Psalms 33:8 says, "Let all the earth fear the Lord; let all the people of the world revere him." Why should we revere our Heavenly Father? Because He created us, He provides for us, He protects us, He heals and comforts us, and He loves us. "For God so loved the world that he gave his one and only Son, that whoever believes in him shall not perish but have eternal life" (John 3:16). Now I ask this: do you look up to your Father? Do you appreciate that He hung the moon, literally? Do you stand in awe of your Father?

In Psalms 5:7, David tells his readers that it was by God's mercy that he came to his Father. He says, "In reverence will I bow down toward your holy temple." And in verse 8, he asks God to lead him in His righteousness. David wanted his Father to know that he looked up to Him and that he appreciated Him and His creation. He stood in awe of his Father. How can we stand in awe of our Father today? We should stand in awe of our Father by loving Him, talking to Him, listening to Him, and singing praises to Him for all He's done for us. The book of Psalms is full of examples of how we can show respect to our Sovereign Lord. Psalms 99:3 and 106:1 say that we should praise His name. Psalms 99:5, 99:9, and 100:2 tell us that we should worship Him. In Psalms 100:1, we are told that telling others is a way to revere the Lord. We should come to Him with thanksgiving on our hearts as told in Psalms 100:4 and 107:8. By listening to our Father, we are showing Him respect also (Isa. 55:3).

Can you imagine feeling unappreciated, unneeded? Our Creator, Provider, Protector, and Healer hurts when we do not show deep respect for all that He has done for us. If we do not show reverence to God, this grieves Him. In Ephesians 4 we are given instructions for Christian living. Most of this list involves respect for others. When we do not respect those around us, it is like we are not respecting our Heavenly Father. This grieves Him. Verse 30 tells us not to grieve the Holy Spirit of God. By showing God reverence, we are equipping our minds to be more respectful to our sisters. We should stand in awe of Him to reflect His light to those around us living in darkness. We should stand in awe of Him to encourage those around us who are struggling to see Him in their life. We should stand in awe of our Father to glorify Him.

I heard a sermon recently that compared Daniel's prayer in Daniel 9 to the Lord's Prayer in Matthew 6:9–13.[xxii] This message reminded me of how my prayer life should be more focused on my Heavenly Father than on me and my needs. In Daniel 9:1–19, Daniel starts his prayer off with humble adoration. He talks to God about God. Not to himself or about himself. He acknowledges God's character and praises Him. In verses 5–15, Daniel gives an honest confession. He confesses the sins of the nation. Sins of wickedness and rebellion, not listening or following commands, shame, unfaithfulness, and the list goes on. In verses 16–19, Daniel pleads with God for a listening ear, for forgiveness, and for mercy. He had a heartfelt petition for the Lord. In verses 16, 17, and 19b, Daniel had a holy motivation. Daniel's motivation was for God's glory, not his. When we go to God in prayer, adoring Him, confessing our sins to Him, asking Him for forgiveness and mercy, and giving Him the glory, we are showing reverence to Him. The wonderful thing about prayer is that we can talk to our Heavenly Father whenever we want to and wherever we are at that moment. He is always listening to our petitions and praises. The more time we spend with God, the closer we come to Him. It becomes easier to be intimate with Him, and through time we grow in appreciation of Him and give Him the glory. As we grow closer to Him and learn to appreciate Him, we are better able to learn how to love and appreciate those around us. We see that God loves us for who He made and does not view us as flawed or failing. It is then that we are able to love others for whom God made them, and we can see past their flaws and failures.

When we allow God to discipline us, we are accepting His training to make us better children of His. He is not punishing us; He is teaching us. The Message translation words this well:

In this all-out match against sin, others have suffered far worse than you, to say nothing of what Jesus went through—all that bloodshed! So don't feel sorry for yourselves. Or have you forgotten how good parents treat children, and that God regards you as his children? My dear child, don't shrug off God's discipline, but don't be crushed by it either. It's the child he loves that he disciplines; the child he embraces, he also corrects. God is educating you; that's why you must never drop out. He's treating you as dear children. This trouble you're in isn't punishment; it's training, the normal experience of children. Only irresponsible parents leave children to fend for themselves. Would you prefer an irresponsible God? We respect our own parents for training and not spoiling us, so why not embrace God's training so we can truly live? While we were children, our parents did what seemed best to them. But God is doing what is best for us, training us to live God's holy best. At the time, discipline isn't much fun. It always feels like it's going against the grain. Later, of course, it pays off handsomely, for it's the well-trained who find themselves mature in their relationship with God. So don't sit around on your hands! No more dragging your feet! Clear the path for long-distance runners so no one will trip and fall, so no one will step in a hole and sprain an ankle. Help each other out. And run for it! (Heb. 12:4–13)

Showing reverence for God is accepting His discipline for us. Once we grasp God's discipline for us, we can be better equipped to practice self-discipline.

Chapter Ten: Reverence for God

Discussion

1) What are some ways that others make you feel more respected?

2) Do you think God would feel respected if you were to do the same for Him?

3) Is reverence for God a one-time event? Why or why not?

Dig deeper

1) Read I Samuel 1:10—11, 15—16; 2:1—11; and I Samuel 3. Hannah had a deep respect for God. She knew that if she poured her heart out to Him long enough, He would listen to her petition. Then, she praised God for what He had done for her. She praised Him for His holiness, that He is all-knowing, all-present, and all-powerful. She fulfilled her promise to God by giving her son over to serve God. Samuel grew up in the house of the LORD and followed God's plan for him. We too can have reverence for God even while living in this world full of sin and disappointments. We must look to Him for guidance, understanding and trust that He will get us through the rough times while praising Him for all He has blessed us with.

2) Mary, a teenager at the time, was told she would be the mother of the Son of God. She was scared and shocked, but she was thankful and willing to be the delivery person of God in the flesh. Read Mary's song of praise in Luke 1:46—55. This is similar to Hannah's prayer of thanksgiving and praise. These ladies are great examples of trusting God completely and praising Him and giving Him all the glory for what He has blessed us all with. We too should "burst with God-news" (v. 46 MSG).

3) Job 1:1 reads: "Job was a man who lived in Uz. He was honest inside and out, a man of his word, who was totally devoted to God and hated evil with a passion" (MSG). Satan noticed Job's respect for God. God allowed Satan to test Job's love and devotion for Him. Did this stop Job from loving God and trusting Him? He did not give up on God. He pleaded with God over and over until God answered. He looked to God for strength to carry him through. God confronted Job in chapter 38—40:2. Job 40:3—5 also states that:v"Job answered: 'I'm speechless, in awe—words fail me. I should never have opened my mouth! I've talked too much, way too much. I'm ready to shut up and listen'" (MSG). Sometimes we must stop and listen to God.

Thoughts to ponder

Jesus was our greatest example of reverence for God. He was God in the flesh and yet He still spent time in prayer and worship to His Father. Read Luke 22:39—46 and meditate on how Jesus looked to His Father at a time when He was so full of sorrow. Jesus knew He was soon to be put through a lot of torture and ridicule. He would ultimately die a very cruel and harsh death after all the beatings, spitting, and mocking. He knew He could call on 10,000 angels to come and rescue Him. He also knew that was not God's plan. He knew by making that decision He would be saved, but none of us would gain eternal life. He took three of His closest friends with Him to the Mount of Olives to pray. He wanted them to watch out for Him and protect Him. Unfortunately, they kept falling asleep. He offered a suggestion to them to get up and pray so they would not be tempted. Are you like these men, so exhausted from life's trials that you fall asleep. Next time life has you down, follow Jesus' suggestion and get up and pray. Thank God for all He has done for you and ask for His strength and guidance. Stand in awe of His glory.

Diving into action

Be intentional in showing your Father your love and appreciation for Him and all He has done.

<u>CHAPTER ELEVEN</u>

Self-Discipline

Self-discipline is an act of cultivation. It requires you to connect today's actions to tomorrow's results. There's a season for sowing [and] a season for reaping. Self-discipline helps you know which is which.
Gary Ryan Blair[xxiii]

Self-Discipline

Before we can be disciplined in an area, we must learn that area. We have discussed ways to be a Dear Sister: by drawing near to God, encouraging others, associating with others, refreshing our spirit of compassion, having a sincere heart, being intimate with God, being a sounding board as we listen to others, spending time together, exhorting one another, and showing reverence to God. I feel that each of these qualities will help us in our walk with God, to bring us closer to Him, help us show others how to come closer to Him, and give Him the glory for all He has done. Once we grasp loving and respecting God, we can work on loving and respecting our sisters. Being a Dear Sister does not happen overnight. It takes time, motivation, and discipline. This chapter will focus on the discipline we need to love others as we love ourselves. "Self-discipline is control over your conscious decisions to do or not to do, speak or not to speak, what you are thinking, and what you are imagining at the time. Self-discipline refers to the mind as it gives commands to the body."[xxiv]

According to 2 Timothy 1:7, God has given us the mind-set to be disciplined in our lives. It is up to us to use this to help us grow closer to each other. As children of God, we have been set free from the bondage of sin. God gave us the Holy Spirit when we chose to become adopted into His family of believers. The Holy Spirit is God living within our hearts, helping us make conscious decisions to help us live freely as His children. Paul explains this to the Christians in Rome in Romans 8. By allowing the Holy Spirit to work in our lives, we are practicing the self-discipline Paul told Timothy about in 2 Timothy 1:7. Galatians 5:23 lists some characteristics we gain from allowing the Holy Spirit to lead us in life. These are love, joy, peace, patience, kindness, goodness, faithfulness, gentleness, and self-control. By living in peace with a joyful heart; by being kind, good, and gentle to our sisters; and by being faithful to them and to God, we are demonstrating love. This all takes self-control—the discipline we need to control our minds to speak, think, and act in a way that is pleasing to God.

In Luke 4:1–13, we see several points about Jesus being self-disciplined that we can relate to and learn from. First, He was full of the Holy Spirit. We, too, are given the Holy Spirit when we become Christians. The Spirit teaches us, builds us up, intercedes for us, and guides us. Second, Jesus allowed the Spirit to lead Him.

We, too, should allow the Spirit to lead us through life. Third, He knew the scriptures and quoted some to Satan each time He was tempted. This is why it is so important for us to draw near to God, become intimate with Him, and show reverence to Him. So we, too, can use the "sword of the Spirit, which is the word of God" (Eph. 6:17) to fight off Satan when he tempts us. Jesus made the conscious decision not to let Satan defeat Him and win this battle. By knowing God's word and following the Holy Spirit's guidance, we too are making a conscious decision not to let Satan defeat us.

When I think of someone from the Bible who was self-disciplined, Daniel comes to mind. In Daniel 1, we read of him making a conscious decision not to eat of the royal food and wine given to him during his training in Babylon. Instead he requested vegetables and water because he knew they were better for his body and overall health. In chapter 2, he made the conscious decision to pray (and ask his friends to pray) for insight from God to interpret the king's dream. And he gave God the glory for the interpretation as well. In chapter 6, Daniel was thrown into a den of lions because of his conscious decision to pray to God and not bow down to the king. Daniel's dedication to his God and his discipline to worship Him daily through prayer allowed him to risk everything, knowing that God would be there with him through it all. Because of his trust in God, he did not view it as a risk. And because of this conscious decision Daniel made, the king and those around were able to witness his devout love for God, and they witnessed God's miraculous rescue for him.

Hebrews 10:23 states, "Let us hold unswervingly to the hope we profess, for He who promised is faithful." If you are driving a car and you swerve off the road, you lose control. Usually when this happens, it is because you are not paying attention or you are distracted. You have to keep your eyes on the road and make conscious decisions while driving. It is the same with life. As we walk down the path of life, we have to pay attention to the path we are taking and to all the surroundings. We have to stay focused on what is ahead of us. We have to make conscious decisions at each intersection, curve, and hill so that our next turn or slope is in the right direction, leading to the right ending of our journey. Hebrews 12 follows the famous "faith chapter." Verses 1 through 13 focus on God disciplining His children. "Let us run the race with perseverance," and "Let us fix our eyes on Jesus." By demonstrating perseverance, we are showing God that we are disciplined. By keeping our focus on Jesus, we are gaining an understanding of His love for us and are better able to let God's light shine to those around us. My prayer for you is that you put these God-given qualities into practice, making a conscious decision to live with greater discipline to aid you in your success as a Dear Sister! Once we make this decision, we must find that motivation to continue on so that we can live the true life.

Chapter Eleven: Self-Discipline

Discussion

1) Discuss ways women can be self-disciplined in everyday life.

2) What stage of life are you in now? Discuss how each stage of life calls for different types of self-discipline to prepare you for the next stage in life.

3) How can you help your sisters be more self-disciplined?

Dig deeper

1) While Proverbs 31:10—31 focuses on a wife of noble character, we can all relate to this woman. Read this passage and write down ways this woman portrayed self-discipline in her life.

2) Paul was converted to Christianity after being blinded by God. He talks in 2 Corinthians 12 about not being worthy to boast except that of boasting of his weaknesses. He was given a thorn in the flesh (v. 7) so that he may rely on God and not himself. Because of this he was glad to be weak. His perseverance to over-come the hard times of persecution, sickness, hard-

ships, imprisonments is the same self-discipline that we should strive for. When you suffer from trials in your life, do you pull your strength from God or do you look to yourself to solve all your problems? Read 2 Corinthians 12:1—10 and strive to "delight" in your weaknesses and trials in life.

3) Read Matthew 25:1—13. There were ten women invited to a wedding party. The groom did not show up when they had expected him to. Five of these women were prepared for his late arrival while the other five were not. Women who are self-disciplined are organized and prepared. Are you prepared? Do you have what you need to keep your light shining for Jesus?

Thoughts to ponder

Esther was a strong woman even if she was scared. As you know, she was Mordecai's niece and became a Queen. She eventually had a decision to make to save not only herself, but her nation. In chapter 3 of the book of Esther we see that Haman did not like that Mordecai was not bowing down to the king. He convinced the king that Mordecai and the other Jews in the area be destroyed. When word got to Esther of this she got word back to Mordecai to tell the Jews in the area to fast for her for three days. Then she went to the king. She spent that time fasting as well. In that time, fasting was not only going without eating, it also included prayer and worship time. Esther spent this time in prayer asking for God's strength and courage to get her through this sticky situation. She knew that going to the king without an invitation could be life-threatening. She also knew that if she trusted in God, He could save her life. It was through intimacy with God and reverence for God that Esther was able to discipline herself to know when to approach the king and how to approach him. Her conscious decisions saved her family-the Jews of Susa.

Diving into action

Take time to reflect on what you have been studying throughout this book and put a plan in place to discipline yourself to follow through with what you have learned.

CHAPTER TWELVE

Dear Sisters: Live the True Life

Infuse your life with action. Don't wait for it to happen. Make it happen. Make your own future. Make your own hope. Make your own love. And whatever your beliefs, honor your Creator, not by passively waiting for grace to come down from upon high, but by doing what you can to make grace happen...yourself, right now, right down here on Earth.

Bradley Whitford[xxv]

CHAPTER TWELVE

Dear Sisters: Live the True Life

A comma is a punctuation mark that continues a sentence. The title of this book is *Dear Sisters*, with the intention of a comma after *Dear Sisters*, suggesting that these words are the salutation of a letter addressed to you and to let you know there is more to the story. As my daughter was preparing to graduate from high school, I thought of the "comma" in her life. Life as she knew it would not continue, but there was a new chapter in her life that she looked forward to and is now enjoying. I have enjoyed being a part of her planning for the future—filling out job applications, college applications, and scholarship applications. We have seen, though, that it takes looking back at her past (but not dwelling on it) to remember her strengths and to see things to work on improving. The applications she was filling out asked questions to help the interviewer get to know her a little better. She had to help them see who she was and what she knew. We, as God's children, do not need to "explain" ourselves to Him. But we do need to show ourselves approved so the world sees who we really are. We need to be true to ourselves and to others so they see Jesus living in us. We too can add a new chapter to our life, bringing life (if you will) to our life. We need to look back only enough to see where we need to make changes. Then, we can move forward and enjoy the true life that God has given us.

An abundant life begins when you draw near to God and is made full by you encouraging and associating with your sisters, refreshing your spirit of compassion, having a sincere heart, listening to and doing things together with your sisters, exhorting your sisters, showing reverence to God, and having self-discipline to follow through with each of these steps to becoming and continuing to be a Dear Sister. As you discipline yourself to be a Dear Sister, you not only grow closer to others and help them grow closer to God, you also grow closer to the Father yourself. You live the full life, a life worthy of the Lord, as it says in Colossians 1:10. You live a worthy life by bearing fruit and growing in the knowledge of God. How did this begin? "For he has rescued us from the dominion of darkness and brought us into the kingdom of the Son he loves, in whom we have redemption, the forgiveness of sins" (Col. 1:13–14). Our true life began with God's true love for us when He sacrificed His one and only Son, and our life continues to be full as we gain a greater understanding of God and live according to this understanding.

The Message Bible words Matthew 5:14–16 so well:

Here's another way to put it: You're here to be light, bringing out the God-colors in the world. God is not a secret to be kept. We're going public with this, as public as a city on a hill. If I make you light-bearers, you don't think I'm going to hide you under a bucket, do you? I'm putting you on a light stand. Now that I've put you there on a hilltop, on a light stand—shine! Keep open house; be generous with your lives. By opening up to others, you'll prompt people to open up with God, this generous Father in heaven.

What a reassurance we have from our Lord to shine for Him! He gives us the light, the source of living. We need to keep it shining for all to see the way to Him.

"But you are a chosen people, a royal priesthood, a holy nation, God's special possession, that you may declare the praises of him who called you out of darkness into his wonderful light" (1 Pet. 2:9). We were created in God's image, and when we chose to follow Him, we became His "special possession." We have been freed from the bondage of sin. Now is our chance to show others who our Creator and King is. We can do this by following 1 Peter 2:17: "Show proper respect to everyone, love the family of believers, fear God, honor the emperor." When we respect others, love others, fear God, and submit to those of authority, we are like living stones. Christ is the cornerstone that holds us together, and we are built into His temple, stone by stone (Eph. 2:19–22). As we go through life, the abundancy of life comes in when we use our life to build His temple with our "living stones." Anyone who has remodeled or built a house knows that it is not a quick and easy process. Those in the midst of the construction get dirty. They work hard and sweat. The area of construction is a mess. But when the process is complete and all the mess has been swept up and wiped clean, there is a great feeling that comes over those who worked so hard. The beauty of the work is seen and appreciated. Our life is the same. It will be messy at times. There is no quick and easy process to living a full life. There will be hard work involved. The messier it starts and the harder one works, the more appreciated the end result is by the worker and the owner. God sees our mess; He understands our hard work. He loves us regardless, but He feels more appreciated and needed when we go to Him with our mess and lean on Him for help. He yearns for us to look to Him for strength and guidance. He desires to be praised. He is filled with joy to see us working together as a family to bring others to Him.

Do you want to live the true life? Paul talks about striving to improve his life in Philippians 3:12–14: "Not that I have already obtained all this, or have already arrived at my goal, but I press on to take hold of that for which Christ Jesus took hold of me. Brothers and sisters, I do not consider myself yet to have taken hold of it. But one thing I do: Forgetting what is behind and straining toward what is ahead, I press on toward the goal to win the prize for which God has called me heavenward in Christ Jesus." My prayer for you is that the passion to live the true life grows within you. May you live in such a way that your Heavenly Father knows your gratefulness for His grace and forgiveness that has brought you to this moment in your life. And as you experience this, may you be passionate about glorifying Him in all you do and shining His love to everyone around you. Finally, my hope is that this book guides you on a journey to seek the high calling of Christ and helps you build a sisterhood to walk through this journey with you. God has worked in me in a mighty way during the writing of this book, and I pray that He uses it in a powerful way to grow you as well to be a Dear Sister to everyone God brings your way.

Chapter Twelve: Dear Sisters, Live the True Life

Discussion

1)   Discuss ways you feel like you are living a true, abundant life.

2)   How do you think God feels knowing you are striving to live the full life He desires for you?

3)   Do others gain from your abundant living? Why or why not?

Dig deeper

1)   Read Joshua 4. What a sense of accomplishment these people must have felt after traveling for so long. They can finally see their destination is so near then God gives Joshua another task. Pick twelve men, one from each tribe and have him find a stone from the dry river bed of Jordan as you are crossing. They were then instructed to carry their chosen stone to the other side of the river. They placed these stones together as a marker to remind their people for generations to come of how God helped them cross the Jordan River. We too should share our life story with our family and friends. This is a great way to give praise and glory to

God and to let others know more about our Provider and Protector. He gets us through any situation that we ask Him to help us through.

2)   In Job 42:17 we read "Job died, an old man and full of years." Job lived a great life for many years. In Job 1:1 we read that he was "blameless and upright; he feared God and shunned evil." If you have not read the story of Job in a while, you may want to read it or listen to it on a Bible App. God allowed Satan to test Job's faithfulness in God. Job was patient as he watched his wealth disappear, lost his family either due to death or disgrace, and his health diminished. He did not give up on God though. He called out to God and constantly sought His favor and help. Let us not give up on life. Seek God's favor and help.

3)   The two greatest commands for us to follow are to love God with all that we have and to love our neighbor as ourselves (Mark 12:33). James 2:8 reminds us of this as the writer says, "If you really keep the royal law found in Scripture, 'Love your neighbor as yourself,' you are doing right." Our sisters are our neighbors. They are also family. We need to love them as we love ourselves. By being a Dear Sister, you are following these commands and you WILL live the true life.

Thoughts to ponder

Paul considered himself the worst of sinners. He had a messy life, but God swept the mess clean and wiped his sins away. He showed mercy to Paul and He shows mercy to us. Read I Timothy 1:16 and meditate on it. What in your life is messy? What do you want God to wipe away? Ask Him to forgive you and start to live a true life today.

Diving into action

Follow God's will for you as you go through life. Make it more abundant with each new day.

APPENDIX

Recipe for a Truly Good Life

Take 12 months—first seeing they are free from old memories of bitterness and hate and jealousy. Cleanse them completely from clinging spite. Pick off all specks of littleness. In short, have these 12 months as clean as when they first came from the storehouse of time.

Cut these months into 30–31 equal parts. This batch will keep just one year. Do NOT make up the whole batch at one time. You can spoil the entire lot this way.

Prepare just one date at a time as follows:

Into each day put equal parts of faith, patience, work, hope, and kindness, with a sprinkling of prayer, tolerance, and rest. To this add a teaspoon of good spirit, fun, and laughter.

Cook thoroughly in fervent heat of good living. Garnish with a few smiles and a spirit of joy. Serve it to your friends and family with unselfishness.

—Author unknown

ABOUT THE AUTHOR

Kaye Mayes is a 1993 graduate of Freed-Hardeman University and has been a member of the Shelby Church of Christ for 20 years. She has taught Bible classes for ages 6 months to adult and has organized several youth and ladies day events, having also been a speaker for the Ladies Day at Shelby Church of Christ. She is also a full-time employee and mom who enjoys spending time helping her husband on their family farm. During her free time, she enjoys spending time with family and friends, spending time out in God's creation, and looking for healthy recipes to prepare for her family.

Endnotes

[i] From Warren W. Wiersbe, *The Integrity Crisis* (Thomas Nelson, 1991), 119, quoted on Bible.org, https://bible.org/illustration/submission-our-nature-god.

[ii] "8 Wonderful Gifts That Don't Cost a Cent," *Home and Garden,* November 30, 2009.

[iii] Acronym by Deri Latimer, http://www.derilatimer.com/t-h-i-n-k-before-you-speak/.

[iv]

[v] "8 Wonderful Gifts."

[vi] Ex. 32:13 referenced from Gen. 15:5 and Gen. 22:17.

[vii] 1 John 4:7–13 (NIV); [sisters] is my paraphrase of "friends."

[viii] Jonathan Lockwood Huie's Friendship Quotes, http://www.quotes-friendship.com/quotes/sincere/.

[ix] "Sincere,"Merriam-Webster.com, Accessed April 28, 2017, https://www.merriam-webster.com/dictionary/sincere.

[x] Walter Bauer, William F. Arndt, F. Wilbur Gingrich, and Frederick W. Danker, *A Greek-English Lexicon of the New Testament and Other Early Christian Literature,* 2nd ed. (Chicago: University of Chicago Press, 1979).

[xi] "Sincere," Accessed April 28, 2017, http://www.latin-dictionary.net/search/latin/sincere.

[xii] "How to Verify the Purity of Honey," *WikiHow,* http://www.wikihow.com/Verify-the-Purity-of-Honey.

[xiii] Timothy Keller, AZ Quotes, http://www.azquotes.com/quote/751682.

[xiv] "8 Wonderful Gifts."

[xv] "8 Wonderful Gifts."

[xvi] *Inspirational Words of Wisdom,* "Henry Ford Quotes," http://www.wow4u.com/henry-ford/index.html.

[xvii] "Community," *Accessed April 28,* 2017, https://www.merriam-webster.com/dictionary/community.

[xviii] *Brainy Quote,* https://www.brainyquote.com/quotes/quotes/c/carlsandbu121886.html?src=t_gentle.

[xix] *Dictionary.com Unabridged,* s.v. "judge," accessed January 28, 2017, http://www.dictionary.com/browse/judge.

[xx] 2 Timothy 3:16, Easy-to-Read Version (ERV), Bible League International, 2006.

[xxi] *Brainy Quote*; read more at https://www.brainyquote.com/search_results.html?q=rever ence.

[xxii] Skip Heitzig, "The Connection," *LightSource*, http://www.lightsource.com/ministry/the-connection/i-dare-you-pray-part-2-daniel-94-19-394441.html.

[xxiii] *Brainy Quote*; read more at https://www.brainyquote.com/search_results.html?q=self-discipline.

[xxiv] *Collinsdictionary.com*, s.v. "self-discipline," accessed April 15, 2017, https://www.collinsdictionary.com/us/dictionary/english/s elf-discipline.

[xxv] *Brainy Quote*; read more at https://www.brainyquote.com/search_results.html?q=life.

Also by Renewed Christian Living

Life is busy. But the everyday rush shouldn't keep us from a deep, moving spirituality. In *Movement: A 40 Day Spiritual Journey*, Matthew Miller invites you on a 40-day devotional expedition towards intentional discipleship amid a culture that never stops. Each day provides busy adults with the opportunity to explore new depths of faith through compassionate change. These devotions will inspire and equip you to rediscover your passion for Christ as you endeavor on your own personal revolution. By embarking on this journey, you will experience inward renewal as you discover and join in the adventure of God's purpose for your life.

(Available at renewedchristianpublishing.com or on Amazon)